SCOTTISH FOOTBALL

A PICTORIAL HISTORY
From 1867 To The Present Day

KEVIN McCARRA

Clydesdale Bank Heritage Series No. 2

Third Eye Centre
and
Polygon Books
1984

SCOTTISH FOOTBALL

A PICTORIAL HISTORY
From 1867 To The Present Day

KEVIN McCARRA

Published September 1984 in an edition of 6,000 copies, of which 1,200 are clothbound and 4,800 paperbacked
Second edition of 4000 copies November 1984
© Third Eye Centre and Kevin McCarra
ISBN 0 904919 88 9 (Cloth)   0 904919 89 7 (Paper)

Clydesdale Bank Heritage Series No. 2

Edited and designed by Christopher Carrell (Third Eye Centre), in association with Alice Bain
Cover design by James Hutcheson

Published by Third Eye Centre (Glasgow) Ltd. and Polygon Books (Edinburgh)
Distributed by Polygon Books, 1 Buccleuch Place, Edinburgh EH8 9LW
Telephone: 031 667 5718
Printed by E.F. Peterson, 12 Laygate, South Shields, Tyne & Wear
Telephone: 0632 563493

Third Eye Centre (Glasgow) Ltd., an independent arts centre with charitable status, is subsidised by the Scottish Arts Council and Glasgow District Council.

Front cover: *Archie Gemmill celebrates his second goal against Holland. World Cup Finals 1978. Colorsport.*

Below: *Drawing of the England v. Scotland match of 1879.*

Contents

Below: *Eric Black scores the first goal in Aberdeen's 1984 Scottish Cup Final victory over Celtic. The ball has bounced behind keeper Bonner's body.*

Preface

On July 13th 1983 Third Eye Centre's exhibition *Scottish Football: a History* was officially opened by one of Scotland's most celebrated footballers, Denis Law, and was on show at the Centre until August 20th. The exhibition was researched by Kevin McCarra, sponsored by Clydesdale Bank, and organised by Third Eye Centre as one of its contributions to Glasgow's year-long "Pride Of the Clyde Celebrations: Welcome Home — Glasgow 1983". Following its Glasgow showing, where it attracted over 30,000 visitors — a record exhibition attendance for Third Eye — *Scottish Football: a History* toured with great success to Edinburgh, Dundee and Aberdeen.

This book by Kevin McCarra has been developed from the exhibition. It is published in association with Clydesdale Bank, without whose whole-hearted financial support neither exhibition nor book could have been brought into existence.

The *Glasgow Herald* generously contributed a large number of photographs to the exhibition, and their generosity has been extended to this book, with the contribution of nearly one hundred photographs from their picture library.

In addition to these two major benefactors many organisations and individuals have also made valuable contributions, and the publishers would like to add their warm thanks to the author's acknowledgements.

Christopher Carrell
Director, Third Eye Centre

Below: *Denis Law soars above England's Bobby Moore. See p.108.*

Acknowledgements

All who assisted in the making of the exhibition *Scottish Football: a History*, in which this book has its origins, are due my sincere thanks in regard to this publication. The scope of the subject matter has led to my inflicting a barrage of questions on a number of experts. Foremost amongst those who must have come to dread the ringing of their phones is Pat Woods. He answered my every question with thoroughness and enthusiasm. Alan Cunningham introduced me to a large number of the people who were able, and willing, to save me from error time and again.

Amongst those individuals who provided information, photographs or general assistance are Alastair Alexander, Ian Archer, Alex Benvie, Graham Blackwood, Jim Blair, Gerard Cairns, Alec Cowie, Bob Crampsey, Alan Dick, Fraser Elder, Alex Hair, Jack Harkness, Jim Hossack, John Hutchinson, Hugh Keevins, Robert Livingstone, Thomas Lochhead, Stewart Marshall, Robert McElroy, Ian McLellan, Rod McLeod, Gerard McNee, Bob McPhail, Andrew Mitchell, Ian Orton, David Richardson, Forrest Robertson, Peter Rundo, Jim Rutherford, Ray Spiller and the Association of Football Statisticians, Molly Stallon, John Stephen, Charles Tennant, David Thomson, Frank Tocher, Michael Tooby, Jack Webster, and Hamish Whyte. The book was largely written in the Glasgow Room of the Mitchell Library and I wish to thank Joe Fisher and his staff whose friendliness and expertise make it a haven. Many hours were spent in the *Glasgow Herald's* picture library, and I would like to thank the library staff, in particular Robert Tweedie, for his patience and advice.

Jack Murray has made the fruits of his many years of collecting available to me. Much of the historic material would surely have been lost without his enthusiasm. Scottish football, in general, owes him a great debt.

Much material has been derived from the clubs and officiating bodies. The following have assisted greatly: the Scottish Football Association, the Scottish Football League, Aberdeen, Arbroath, Celtic, Dumbarton, Dundee United, East Fife, Heart of Midlothian, Partick Thistle, Queen's Park, Rangers and St. Mirren.

Many bodies have loaned material or given permission to reproduce it. Acknowledgements are due to *Aberdeen Evening Express*, Colorsport, *Daily Express*, *Daily Record* and *Sunday Mail*, Dumbarton District Libraries, *Edinburgh Evening News*, *Glasgow Herald*, the People's Palace (Glasgow), Sportapics, Sports Projects, and Syndication International.

I wish to thank two people, outside Third Eye Centre, who assisted in the production of this book. George Oliver did an enormous amount of photographic work and met the unreasonable deadlines imposed without ever losing his celebrated good humour. Susan Stewart endured a disrupted social life as a result of this work but remained totally enthusiastic about it. She also spent countless hours in the numbing process of weeding this book of errors. Any that remain are, of course, solely my own responsibility.

Kevin McCarra

For my father, Joseph McCarra

Introduction

It was my great-uncle, Giuseppe Filippi, who took me to my first football match. In the second half a star player who was playing out the last days of a great career was brought on as substitute. Almost immediately, a corner was awarded and he gently jogged across, as if the game was of limitless duration, to take it. After much signalling and deployment of forces, he stepped forward and cuffed the ball into the side netting, out of play. The sheer foolishness of it stifled anger and, a little later, it was remembered as part of the entertainment.

Another time, I was watching a pre-season friendly at Lesser Hampden, part of an attendance that would have compared unfavourably with a normal bus queue. At one point a Queen's Park forward gathered the ball with his back to goal but contrived to turn and slip his marker. With customary optimism, generally unsupported by co-ordination of eye and foot, he let fly from some thirty yards. There is a 'sweet spot' on the face of the golf club which when it catches the ball will send it soaring away, making it appear even to accelerate in its rising trajectory. Feet have them too and only the net broke the shot's glorious flight. The scorer and the crowd knew something marvellous had occurred.

Both of these memories are as clear in my mind as any of the others I have of watching the sport but neither would ever feature in any list of football's great moments. This is the problem with histories of football. They can never hope to recall all, or even the majority, of its readers' fondest memories.Nor is it simply a matter of being unable to include obscure memories of great players or vital moments from minor games. The winning of a lesser division is almost certainly as great an achievement as the acquisition of a prestigious trophy by one of the game's giants, but it is bound to be given short shrift in a book which aims to cover the events of well over a century's play in a limited number of pages. One can only ever write *a* history of the game, never *the* history and, furthermore, this is a *pictorial* history.

For all that, I believe the reader will find great variety within this book, since the pictorial format allows an author to deal economically with his subject. What need for lengthy praise of, for example, Denis Law's graceful athleticism when a photograph shows him poised in mid-air, far above the hapless Bobby Moore? Nor is it simply the action shots which tell a story. The length of shorts and cumbersomeness of boots worn by the footballers in old team group photos suggest a whole vanished style of play.

It is my hope that this book will not only constitute a vivid record of the past but also encourage our enthusiasm for the current game, the game for which Saturdays were invented.

Kevin McCarra

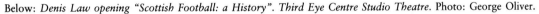

Below: *Denis Law opening "Scottish Football: a History". Third Eye Centre Studio Theatre.* Photo: George Oliver.

5

Glasgow 9th July 1867

Tonight at half past eight o'clock a number of gentlemen met at No. 3 Eglinton Terrace for the purpose of forming a "Football Club". — After Mr. Black was called to the Chair a good deal of debating ensued and ultimately the following measures were voted for and carried, viz

First.	That the Club should be called the 'Queen's Park Football club'. —
Second.	That there should be four office bearers viz a President, Captain, Secretary and Treasurer —
Third	That there should be thirteen members of Committee including Office Bearers seven of whom to form a quorum

the following gentlemen were then duly elected as Officebearers and members of Committee viz

1	Mr Ritchie, President	9	Mr Edminston M of C
2	„ Black, Captain:	10	„ P Davidson —
3	„ Klinger, Secretary:	11	„ Gladstone —
4	„ Smith Sr Treasurer.	12	„ Reid —
5	„ Grant, Mem of Committee	13	„ Skinner —
6	„ Gardner Sr —		
7	„ Davidson R. —		
8	„ Smith Jr. —		

The Secretary then gave intimation that the Committee would meet on the 15th inst for further deliberation and to draw out a code of rules for the guidance of the Club. The Business for the evening being now finished the members retired after awarding a hearty vote of thanks to Mr. Black for his able conduct in the chair.

W. M. Klinger
Secrty.

Lewis L. Black
Chairman.

FIRST MINUTE, 1867.

Above: *Minutes of the meeting at which Queen's Park were formed, 9th July 1867.*

Below: *Letter from Queen's Park Secretary, Robert Gardner, arranging the first known game between two Scottish clubs.*

Dear Sir,

I duly received your letter dated 25th inst. on Monday Afternoon, but as we had a Committee Meeting called for this evening at which time it was submitted, I could not reply to it earlier. I have now been requested by the Committee, on behalf of our Club, to accept the challenge you kindly sent, for which we have to thank you, to play us a friendly Match at Football on our Ground, Queen's Park, at the hour you mentioned, on Saturday, first proximo, with twenty players on each side. We consider, however, that Two-hours is quite long enough to play in weather such as the present, and hope that this will be satisfactory to you. We would also suggest that if no Goals be got by either side within the first hour, that goals be then exchanged, the ball, of course, to be kicked of from the centre of the field by the side who had the origanal Kick-off, so that boath parties may have the same chance of wind and ground, this we think very fare and can be arranged on the field before beginning the Match. Would you also be good enough to bring your ball with you in case of any breake down, and thus prevent interuptsion. Hoping the weather will favour the Thistle and Queen's.

I remain,

Yours very truly,

(Sgd.) Robt. Gardner

Secy.

The Game Begins
1867 – 1900

The young gentlemen who met at No. 3 Eglinton Terrace on the 9th July 1867 were in some doubt as to the rules of Association Football and, after some discussion, decided to defer a decision on the matter. A copy of the rules was obtained from the Notts. cricketer James Lillywhite, and the gentlemen adapted them to their liking. We have, since those days, become rather more certain about all matters connected with the game.

The business of that evening was the foundation of Queen's Park F.C. – the first great Scottish club. No doubt, however, that year also saw the formation of many other societies devoted to a variety of leisure pursuits. Equally certainly most of them passed quickly into oblivion. Why then did Queen's Park prosper? Why does the 9th July 1867 mark the beginning of our national sport; a sport which, for more than a hundred years, has been a focus of the energies and aspirations of the nation?

The answer lies, firstly, with the shifts in population which occurred in the 19th century. As Scotland became more and more industrialised the work-force and their families tended to be concentrated close to the manufacturing industries. In Glasgow the overcrowding led, in 1866, to the introduction of a system of "Ticketed Housing". In certain areas each tenement was licensed for a fixed maximum number of residents. Nor were these conditions to change quickly. Even in the early 1970s Glasgow's population (896,000) was twice that of Edinburgh, although the two cities occupy comparable areas. These densely packed streets did more than ensure the existence of a potential audience, their squalor guaranteed that their inhabitants would welcome the kind of engrossing and fundamentally simple entertainment football could provide. The growth of the newspaper industry and the development of a public transport system made sure that those people both knew about matches and were able to get to them.

The gradual shortening of the working week was the final necessary ingredient. In the 1860s and '70s the practice of working for only a half-day on Saturday had become unexceptional.

Life is difficult for the pioneer. In Queen's Park's early games both sides were composed of the club's own members, and a certain desperate ingenuity was required if monotony was to be staved off. At one point "Smokers" played "Non-smokers". It must have been with some relief that the Queen's Park Secretary, Robert Gardner, wrote his courteous letter accepting the challenge of a team named Thistle (no relation). The novelty of this fixture may be judged from the fact that it was necessary for Gardner to suggest a few basic rules. The match took place in August 1868, and Queen's Park won.

They continued to do so for many years. Indeed, they were a force in the British Isles. They reached the Final of the F.A.Cup in 1883-84 and again the following season. Blackburn Rovers were the victors on both occasions, but the team was good enough for that first defeat to cause much vexation. The club deplored the judgement of the referee (the spendidly titled Major Marindin) and their fans abominated the team selection.

However, it has to be admitted that football began in England. There, in the late 1840s, a codified version of the wild forms of football which had been known for centuries began to appear. The Football Association was formed in London in 1863 and the F.A. Cup was instituted in 1871.

Below: Mock obituary which appeared in a newspaper following Queen's Park's defeat in the F.A. Cup Final of 1884. The biblical quotation refers to the controversy surrounding team selection.

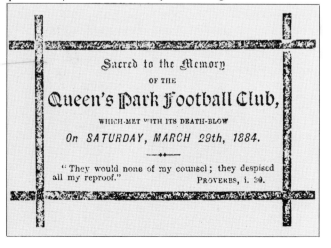

Sacred to the Memory
OF THE
Queen's Park Football Club,
WHICH MET WITH ITS DEATH-BLOW
On SATURDAY, MARCH 29th, 1884.

"They would none of my counsel; they despised all my reproof." PROVERBS, i. 30.

Above: *Charles Alcock, Secretary of the F.A., who organised the first, unofficial, internationals.*

Above: *First official picture of a Scotland team, 1873. A photographer had attended the Hamilton Crescent match of 1872, but he left when the players would not promise to purchase prints from him.*

Right: *Sketches at the first international, Glasgow. The Graphic.*

Below: *Ticket for first official international, 30th November, 1872.*

The concept of international football was an inevitable consequence of the growth of club football. In November 1870 the Secretary of the F.A., Charles Alcock, wrote to the *Glasgow Herald* expressing a desire to arrange matches between Scottish and English players. Four such matches took place in London with Alcock selecting both sides. The Scottish teams, composed of Anglo-Scots, failed to win any of them. The "Alcock Internationals" have no official standing and it was in 1872 that international football truly began.

In that year Queen's Park arranged an international with England and so, before there was any Scottish Football Association, there was battle with our ancient rivals. The priorities of our game were established. The Scotland team, naturally composed of Queen's men, played the game on the 30th November at the Hamilton Crescent cricket ground in Glasgow. The match ended in a goalless draw, but it was said that Scotland deserved a win. That judgement has an infuriatingly familiar ring to it. The Scottish team (which was listed in 2:2:6 formation) was: Robert Gardner; William Ker and J. Taylor; J.J.Thomson and James Smith; Robert Smith, Robert Leckie, Alex Rhind, W. McKinnon, J.B.Weir and D. Wotherspoon.

Football prospered in Britain in the 1870s. The Welsh F.A. was formed in 1876 and they played their first international that same year, losing 4–0 to Scotland in Glasgow. The Irish F.A. was formed in 1880 but did not play its first international until 1882. Any hesitation they may have felt proved to be justified when England won that first match by 13 goals to nil. The Home International Championship began in 1884 and Scotland, with victories over the other three nations, won it.

The financial health of that first international of 1872 was of some consequence. 4,000 people attended and a profit of £33 was generated for Queen's Park. The sport, clubs must have sensed, had a future.

A national organisation was bound to follow. It did so when a meeting called by Queen's Park in March 1873 led both to the institution of a Challenge Cup (the Scottish Cup) and to the formation of the S.F.A. The clubs whose representatives attended that first crucial meeting were: Queen's Park, Clydesdale, Vale of Leven, Dumbreck, Third Lanark Rifle Volunteer Reserves, Eastern, Granville, and Rovers.

At this stage, the whole character of the sport was in the melting pot. The fan in those early days watched a game which included a certain amount of handling and which used touch-downs to determine the result when the match had been drawn in terms of goals. It was difficult for some teams to adapt to the Association Rules which governed the Scottish Cup. On the first day of competition for the trophy, October 18th 1873, Renton played a tie with Kilmarnock on Queen's Park's ground at Crosshill. The account of that game tells us much about the nature of football at that time.

Renton were at a great advantage owing to some of the "Auld Killies" men persistently using their hands, which "is not allowed according to Association Rules." The fact that Kilmarnock were playing with only 10 men probably did their cause no good. The reporter for the *Glasgow News* seems to have been at a loss to describe the events of the match — all the useful clichés that have grown with the game were unavailable to him. Here is Renton's first goal:

"... by well-concentrated rushes, and the skilful dribbling of Kennedy, the Renton eleven soon carried the ball

KEEPING WARM

NEMO ME IMPUNE &c

A HARD STRUGGLE

DRIBBLING

WELL KICKED

SOFT FALLING, FORTUNATELY

HOW'S THAT UMPIRE

WELL DONE MAC!!

SKETCHES AT THE INTERNATIONAL FOOTBALL MATCH, GLASGOW

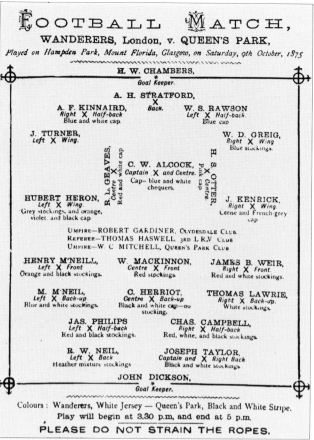

FOOTBALL MATCH,

WANDERERS, London, v. QUEEN'S PARK,

Played on Hampden Park, Mount Florida, Glasgow, on Saturday, 9th October, 1875.

H. W. CHAMBERS,
Goal Keeper.

A. H. STRATFORD,
Back.

A. F. KINNAIRD,
Right X Half-back
Blue and white cap.

W. S. RAWSON
Left X Half-back.
Blue cap.

J. TURNER,
Left X Wing.

W. D. GREIG,
Right X Wing
Blue stockings.

R. L. GEAVES, *Centre — Red and white cap*

C. W. ALCOCK,
Captain X and Centre.
Cap— blue and white chequers.

H. S. OTTER, *Centre — Pink cap.*

HUBERT HERON,
Left X Wing.
Grey stockings, and orange, violet, and black cap.

J. KENRICK,
Right X Wing.
Cerise and French-grey cap

*Umpire—*ROBERT GARDINER, CLYDESDALE CLUB.
*Referee—*THOMAS HASWELL, 3RD L.R.V. CLUB
*Umpire—*W. C. MITCHELL, QUEEN'S PARK CLUB

HENRY M'NEILL,
Left X Front
Orange and black stockings.

W. MACKINNON,
Centre X Front
Red stockings.

JAMES B. WEIR,
Right X Front.
Red and white stockings.

M. M'NEIL,
Left X Back-up.
Blue and white stockings.

C. HERRIOT,
Centre X Back-up.
Black and white cap—no stocking.

THOMAS LAWRIE,
Right X Back-up.
White stockings.

JAS. PHILIPS,
Left X Half-back.
Red and black stockings.

CHAS. CAMPBELL,
Right X Half-back.
Red, white, and black stockings.

R. W. NEIL,
Left X Back
Heather mixture stockings

JOSEPH TAYLOR,
Captain and X Right Back
Black and white stockings.

JOHN DICKSON,
Goal Keeper.

Colours : Wanderers, White Jersey — Queen's Park, Black and White Stripe.
Play will begin at 3.30 p.m., and end at 5 p.m.

PLEASE DO NOT STRAIN THE ROPES.

Above: *Match card of 1875. Queen's Park beat this crack English side 5-0.*

Below: *Vale of Leven, Scottish Cup-winners from 1877 to 1879. Johnny Ferguson is holding the Cup.*

Top right: *Queen's Park, winners of the first Scottish Cup in 1874. Back row L. to R.: A. McKinnon, J. Dickson, T. Lawrie, C. Campbell, R. Neill.*
Front row: R. Leckie, J. Taylor, H. McNeil, J. Thomson, J. Weir, W. McKinnon.

Bottom right: *Arbroath at the time of their 36-0 victory over Aberdeen Bon Accord, 1885.*
Back row L. to R.: R. Tait (Match Secretary), W. Collie, J. Christie (Vice President), E. Doig, C. Mitchell (President), G. Campbell, C. Martin (Treasurer).
Centre row: W. Leslie, H. Rennie, J. Milne, J. Sime, D. Crawford.
Front row: J. Petrie, S. Buick, J. Buick.
Petrie, the club's outside-right, scored thirteen goals in the match.

10

through the Kilmarnock goal-posts."

The impression that physical strength had much to do with this score persists, but little else is communicated Kilmarnock went down by two goals to nil.

To the modern eye the football of the time appears as an alien but rather intriguing world. The following brief portrait of Robert Smith, a Queen's Park player and a member of that first international side, both perplexes and enchants:

". . . very quick but wide dribbler; charges heavily, rather much so; did a good deal for Football Association in Glasgow in his day; gone to the Rocky Mountains."

Football retained an aura of the exotic and wildly unpredictable for quite some time. In a first round Scottish Cup-tie in 1885 Arbroath beat Aberdeen Bon Accord by 36 goals to nil. There must have been something in the air on the East coast that day, for a mere 18 miles away Dundee Harp recorded a 35–0 win over Aberdeen Rovers in the same competition.

Queen's Park won that first Scottish Cup of season 1873-74, by beating Clydesdale by two goals to nil. For good measure they won it in the next two seasons as well. Fine team though they must have been, these victories came rather too easily for the health of the game. In the seventeen matches it took them to do it they scored forty-three goals and conceded four.

The events which finally ended their monopoly took place in front of a small crowd on a wet afternoon late in 1876. Queen's Park opened the scoring in a fifth round match against Vale of Leven through J.B. Weir – a man termed "Prince of the Dribblers" by the English. A shot by the same player seemed certain to tie matters up when it received a fatal deflection from an umpire's umbrella. This mishap requires some explanation. Umpires (one in each half) were appointed by the competing clubs; the referee adjudicated between them. They were not banished to the role of linesmen until 1891. Suspicion must exist that the decisive umbrella was giving shelter to the Vale of Leven appointee. In any case, Queen's eventually lost 2-1.

Further controversy arose when the losers found what they took to be spike marks on the pitch – spikes were strictly illegal. A lengthy correspondence between the clubs, written in tones of gentlemanly accusation, proved inconclusive. One writer in a newspaper sardonically suggested that the offending marks were the product of crows' feet and the match became known as the "Crows' Feet Match". Competition had entered Scottish Football.

Vale of Leven went on to win the trophy and they retained it in the two seasons which followed. The feat was honoured by the presentation of a "loving cup" and the players continued to celebrate their success until well into the 1920s.

By the late 1870s some measure of tactical knowledge and self-awareness seems to have arrived. Vale of Leven certainly knew how to play to their strengths. They beat the English team Wanderers by three goals to one at the Kennington Oval in April 1878 and all three were scored by Ferguson (a man fast enough to win a mile event at Powderhall).

The events of more modern times make it particularly interesting that the Vale's opponents in two of those Cup successes were Rangers. Rangers were formed in the year 1872 (not, as is often said, 1873) by a group of young men who spent their leisure time at Glasgow Green. The nucleus of the club was the McNeil brothers — members of a Gareloch family who had moved to the city — and it was one

Above: *Thomas Vallance, captain of Rangers in the 1870s.*
Below: *Advert for restaurant owned by Vallance.*

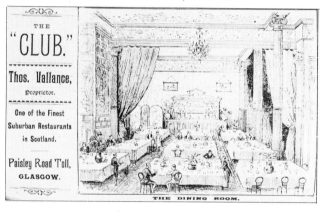

Below: *Renton, Cup-winners and "Champions of the World" in 1888. The players in the team group are, second row, L. to R.: R. Kelso, A. Hannah, J. Lindsay, A. McCall, D. McKechnie.*
Front row: N. McCallum, H. Campbell, J. McCall, J. McNee, J. Kelly, J. Campbell.

of these, Moses, who gave the club its name. Their team in the 1870s was a difficult one to beat; their defence being particularly sound. Their most notable player was, perhaps, their full-back, Tom Vallance – a future President of the club and a considerable businessman. He excelled in athletics as well as football and was, in fact, much stronger than his tall, thin frame suggested. The solidity of his tackling conclusively proved the appearance deceptive.

The two matches with Vale of Leven were bound to have their element of controversy. In the Final of 1877 the first match was fairly quietly drawn but the second (another 1-1 draw) produced a goal by Rangers which was disallowed and a crowd invasion. In the third match a goal by Moses McNeil put his side into a 2-1 lead. They eventually succumbed to the Vale's greater strength, however, and were edged out by three goals to two.

The Final of 1879 drew a crowd large enough to cause the partial collapse of a section of the pavilion. In the game itself, Struthers seemed to have added to his first goal to put Rangers two ahead. The 'goal' was disallowed for off-side, however, and the decision stood despite the incensed reaction of the Rangers players. It seemed that none of this would matter when Rangers entered the last few minutes with their lead intact. Then Ferguson scrambled the ball past a static goalkeeper with only three minutes left and the Vale had won a reprieve. Rangers refused to appear for the replay and the Vale were awarded the Cup.

Nothing of any value can now be said concerning the refereeing of that particular match but there can be little doubt that the referees of the time left much to be desired. The concept of impartiality, for example, seems to have been a sickly and undernourished child. One reels in horror (or amusement) at the thought of the events which must have provoked the statement on referees which is included in the S.F.A. Secretary's report for season 1879-80:

"They should never appear as a twelfth player in a team, or the coacher of any side."

Vale of Leven were, however, the team of the day, and it can hardly be coincidental that Dunbartonshire clubs enjoyed great success in the period. Local rivalry must have produced a considerable incentive to succeed. Dumbarton's one Scottish Cup success occurred in 1883. They were knocked out of the Cup in the first round the following season (1883-84) by their local rivals Renton.

The 1888 Cup victory led to Renton playing the English Cup-winners of that year, West Bromwich Albion, and beating them 4–1 in the midst of a snowstorm. The clubs had agreed that the match should be billed as a "Championship of the World" and the Dunbartonshire side gained that eerie but possibly justified title.

They were not, however, the first Scottish side to lay claim to it. Hibernian had beaten Preston in a similarly titled match the previous year. Of rather more significance, though, is the fact that Hibs had gained sufficient stature to even play such a fixture.

Even the most cursory study of the lists of winners of the Scottish trophies is apt to induce a sense of claustrophobia. It is, therefore, with a sense of gladness that one notes that the Cup at last left the West of Scotland in 1887. Hibs were the winners that year and matters connected with the event make that victory particularly worthy of note.

Most reports give Willie Groves as the scorer of the game's key goal. He took off on a solo run, they say, which

J. HUTCHISON , J. McAULAY , A. LAWRANCE , P. MILLER , A. KENNEDY , M. PATON , L. KEIR .

R. BROWN   R. BROWN   J. LINDSAY   J. MILLER , F. McARTHUR , R. ANDERSON .

Above: *Dumbarton, Cup-winners of 1883.*
Back row, L. to R.: I. Hutchison, J. McAulay, A. Lawrance, P. Miller, A. Kennedy, M. Paton, L. Keir.
Front row: R. Brown ("The Plumber"), R. Brown ("The Sparrow"), J. Lindsay, J. Miller, F. McArthur, R. Anderson.

Below: *Hibs in 1876.*

carried him clear of the defence and calmly slipped the ball past the keeper for the decisive goal. Groves, then, was an important player, but he was also a controversial one.

Teams of the time were required to be of an amateur nature but the clubs were allowed to recompense players for wages lost through taking time off from their 'real' jobs. The system was eminently exploitable and thoroughly exploited. Groves, a stone-mason to trade, was accused just before the Final of being a professional. Vale of Leven even used the services of a private detective to investigate his status. Tensions of this sort were bound to produce a change in the game and, in due course, they did.

In any case, the crowd of 2,000 which greeted the Hibs team at Waverley Station would have had little time for such questions.

The Cup's sojourn in the East was short-lived but there was at least the interest, in 1889, of seeing Third Lanark, who had been in existence for 17 years, at last taking the trophy after having fallen at the final hurdle on two previous occasions. Sadly for the now defunct "Hi Hi" this victory tends to be referred to as Celtic's first Cup Final.

Celtic had been formed in 1887, although they did not play their first game till the following year, as a charitable institution devoted to helping the poor of the East End of Glasgow. The vast support they enjoyed quickly ensured that they would also have the same aims as any large football club. The interest they kindled, indeed, greatly boosted attendances throughout football. The likelihood of success must have been apparent from the start for they drew to their ranks, for their first match, experienced players from

Above: *Willie Groves. Following the 1887 Cup Final an S.F.A. committee met to discuss Groves's amateur status. Only the casting vote of the Chairman saw him declared innocent of the charge of being a professional.*

teams such as Hibs, Renton and Dumbarton. As a club they were to know no infancy.

The game itself had rapidly grown to a position of some importance in the community. Certain key facts could not be ignored. Some teams, it was obvious, were much richer and better supported than others. The presence of a large audience meant that some form of reliable fixture list was needed, since the profusion of friendlies and minor competitions inevitably led to late cancellations and consequent vexations for fans. In the face of these considerations it was hardly surprising that the setting up of a Qualifying Cup to regulate entry to the Scottish Cup was proposed at the S.F.A.'s Annual General Meeting of 1890. This was correctly regarded as a move towards the élitism of a League and the proposal was defeated. The matter, however, was never likely to rest there.

In that same year eleven clubs formed a Scottish League. They were Abercorn, Cambuslang, Celtic, Cowlairs, Dumbarton, Hearts, Rangers, Renton, St. Mirren, Third Lanark, and Vale of Leven. They were met with a barrage of criticism and vilification. Rather bewilderingly, they were faced with accusations of, on the one hand, greed and, on the other, incompetence.

The following quotation from *Scottish Sport* may serve as an example of the kind of passions aroused by the prospect of League football. The League's newly announced rules concerning professionalism are under discussion:

"Our first and last objection to them is that they exist. The entire rules stink of finance — money making and money grabbing."

Left: *Third Lanark, Cup-winners of 1889.*
Back row L. to R.: A. Thompson, R. Downie, J. Rae.
Second back row: J. Marshall, J. Thomson (the club's umpire), R. McFarlane, A. Lochhead, W. French (Match Secretary), J. Hannah.
Centre row: John Oswald, W. Brown (President), W. Johnstone.
Front row: James Oswald, J. Auld.

Below: *Celtic in the year of their first match, 1888.*
Back row L. to R.: J. Anderson (Trainer), J. Quillan, D. Malloy, J. Glass, J. McDonald (Committee Member).
Second row: J. O'Hara, W. McKillop (Committee Member).
Centre row: W. Groves, T. Maley, P. Gallacher, W. Dunning, W. Maley, M. Dunbar.
Front row: J. Coleman, J. McLaren, J. Kelly, N. McCallum, M. McKeown.

Above: *D. McArthur. Celtic's star goalkeeper in the 1890s. In view of the fact that he was only 5ft. 5in. tall his success was remarkable.*

Below: *Celtic Players of 1891. From* Heads and Tales of the Scottish League (No 2).

The actual progress of the League competition in that season was also troubled. A League which had, at the outset, eleven teams, ran from August 16th 1890 to May 21st 1891. The first three months of the season were rendered almost useless by a prolonged spell of bad weather. If that were not enough, the League also had to face difficulties of an internal nature. Celtic, Third Lanark and Cowlairs each had four points deducted from their total for infringements of registration rules and Renton were suspended from the League after playing a game against St. Bernards, weakly disguised as "Edinburgh Saints", who had been branded as professional and accordingly outlawed.

The League's one stroke of good fortune lay in the climax of the competition itself. As the end of the season approached Rangers beat Dumbarton and thus joined them at the top of the table. When they were still level after completing their fixtures it was decided that a play-off was required. That game, on Third Lanark's ground, saw Rangers take a two goal lead, but Dumbarton eventually pulled matters back to level terms. It was agreed that the two teams should be declared joint champions. It is the only time in the game's history that this has happened.

A publication of that year, *Heads and Tales of the Scottish League*, gives the following details concerning the top of the table (the play-off is included):

CLUB.	MATCHES.				POINTS.	GOALS.	
	Played.	Won.	Lost.	Drawn.		Won.	Lost.
Dumbarton,	19	13	2	4	30	63	23
Rangers,	19	13	2	4	30	60	27
Celtic,	18	11	4	3	21	48	21
Cambuslang,	18	8	6	4	20	47	42
3rd L.R.V.,	18	8	7	3	15	38	39
Heart of Midlothian,	18	6	10	2	14	31	37
Abercorn,	18	5	11	2	12	36	47
Vale of Leven,	18	5	12	1	11	27	65
St. Mirren,	18	5	12	1	11	39	62
Cowlairs,	18	3	11	4	6	24	50

From the Celtic, 3rd L.R.V., and Cowlairs, four points each were deducted for infringements of the Registration Rule.

JNO. H. M'LAUGHLIN, *Hon. Secy.*

The numbers of goals scored and conceded were recorded merely as matters of interest; neither goal difference nor goal advantage played any part in determining League position.

It is hardly surprising that the Secretary of the League, in his report at the end of the first season, singled out that League decider for particular praise. It must have regained public attention at the end of an unduly prolonged first campaign. With the benefit of hindsight, however, it seems obvious that the League would survive and, indeed, prosper. It was an immediately viable proposition. Those who attended the first A.G.M. on June 5th 1891 in the Union Hotel, Dunlop Street, Glasgow, heard that there was a balance of £62. 7s on the year's business. *Heads and Tales of the Scottish League* also bears witness to the faith the commercial world had in the fledgling organisation — it is crammed with adverts.

The institution of a League was only the first stage in a process of evolution. Professionalism was bound to come. Although only recognised in England since 1885 it had in

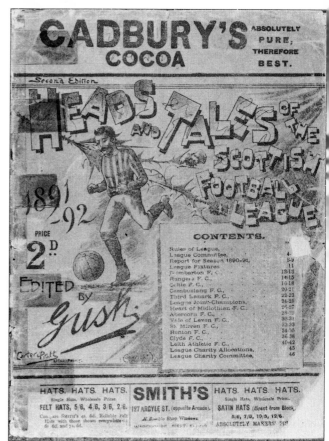

Above: *Front cover of* Heads and Tales of the Scottish League (No. 2).

Below: *Advert from* Heads and Tales of the Scottish League (No. 2).

DUMBARTON.   RANGERS.

Season 1890-91.   Season 1890-91.

JOINT CHAMPIONS OF LEAGUE.

Above: *The joint champions at the conclusion of the first season of League football: From* Heads and Tales of the Scottish League *(No. 2).*

fact been rife for many years before. Naturally, many players were lost from the Scottish game. In their formative years, for example, Rangers lost four fine players to England. The problem was widespread throughout Scottish clubs and the figure of the English scout began to appear as something less than human in the eyes of the Scottish football fan:

"In the meantime, however, the English professional agent, who had been prowling through the ranks of the 'Light Blues', found a willing victim in Wyllie." *Heads and Tales,* 1891.

If money was to become available to Scottish clubs there could be no doubt that they would use it to retain good players. It was not long before money did become available.

In winning the first League championship Rangers made a profit of around £500. Celtic guaranteed the continuation of an already considerable support by winning the Cup in 1892. They did so with a thumping 5-1 victory over Queen's Park, after the first game (a mere 1-0 victory) had been declared void following protest about crowd encroachment on the pitch. The following season they took the League. At New Year 1889 Celtic, although only in their first season, drew a crowd of around 16,000 to their game with Corinthians. By 1890 Celtic were drawing upwards of £5,000 a year, and in 1891 they were sufficiently wealthy to disburse £545 to charity. Nor were Celtic and Rangers the only clubs with earning capacity. Football as a whole was a money-making enterprise. The Glasgow Charities Cup raised over £10,000 for various charitable purposes between 1877 and 1890.

The advocates of amateurism battled hard to retain the status quo. At the A.G.M. of the S.F.A. in 1893, however, professionalism was finally legalised. Amateurism is, of course, a noble cause, but, whatever the rights and wrongs of the matter, it was one which had been lost before what seemed to be the battle had even begun.

A sub-committee of the S.F.A. looked into the matter in 1891 and declared that professionalism was already rampant. On several occasions the S.F.A. called in clubs' books for inspection but since it was common practice to maintain two sets (the real and the fake) this had little effect.

The case of Heart of Midlothian may be taken as typical. Having lost Ross, Ferguson, Brogan, Renwick, Scotland and others, Hearts became very eager to retain their more accomplished players. They were able to sign Maxwell and McNee from the Cartvale Club by promising to pay them. In McNee's case the Hearts Secretary paid 25/- a week to George Barbour, with whom McNee lodged, and Barbour passed the money on to the player. It is said that Barbour told McNee that the money was a gift which arrived with the supplies delivered by a Hearts-supporting grocer. The story goes that McNee maintained a fruitless watch for the delivery boy, but I think we may take leave to doubt it.

Hearts were found out in 1884; they were suspended and the two ex-Cartvale players disqualified for two years. All parties concerned, however, would have been right in thinking that they were simply unlucky to have been caught in what was normal practice. *Scottish Sport's* allegation, in its October 14th 1892 issue, that one club had paid £1,150 in wages the previous season would have startled no-one.

Professionalism arrived, and at the end of the first season of it the Secretary of the League (John H. McLaughlin of Celtic) declared that it has been "a boon to us all". He cited the revival of Dumbarton as proof of this. The loss of players which amateurism made inevitable had previously sent them into rapid decline. The future for small clubs in general was perhaps less bright, however.

The League, too, had grown strong. The balance for the year 1893-94 was £386-0-1, and £200 was donated to charity. The growth in number of the League's members also demonstrates its development. By season 1893-94 it had twenty clubs and operated two divisions.

The 1890s was a period of rapid growth for football. By 1892 the pitch markings bore a fair resemblance to those in use today. Goal nets arrived and were first seen in Scotland in a friendly at Celtic Park on New Year's Day 1892. Much attention has been given to the fact that Celtic the following year played an evening match under lights strung across and above the pitch. Amazingly enough, however, the practice was already familiar. Indeed, as early as October 25th 1878 Third Lanark played a friendly against Vale of Leven at First Cathkin with the aid of artificial lighting. Grounds, too, were developed — one might note, for example, Partick Thistle's achievement in building their Meadowside Stadium.

The game had always been controversial but the introduction of the penalty kick in the summer of 1891 must have helped to raise the temperature a few degrees further. The first in the Scottish League was scored by Archibald McCall on 22nd August 1891 for Renton in a match against Leith at Bank Park, Leith.

The last decade of the 19th century saw Celtic and Rangers complete the process of becoming the game's biggest names. Celtic, with a carefully structured passing game said to be based on that of Preston North End, took four League titles and three Scottish Cups while, in the same period, Rangers won three Leagues and three Cups.

The Ibrox side took the title in season 1898-99 by winning all eighteen games in which they played. Disaster beckoned at Easter Road when their recovery from a two goal deficit had only brought matters to 3-3 in the last minute. A penalty in the final seconds, however, produced the victory. Their Secretary of the time, William Wilton, was also Secretary of the League and he was forced to give a rather bashful eulogy of his own team in his report at the A.G.M.

The sport's claims to full national significance were strengthened by the fact that the 1896 Final involved no West of Scotland club. More than that, for the only time ever the Final was contested outside Glasgow. It took place on Logie Green, home of the Edinburgh team, St. Bernards. There had been fears that the ground could not safely hold a large crowd but, in the event, no harm came to the 16,034 spectators, who watched an engrossing match between Hearts and Hibs. Hearts weathered an early storm before their half-back line of Begbie, Russell and Hogg took control and paved the way for a 3-1 victory.

It was a good period for Hearts since they also won the Cup in 1891, and took the League in 1894-95, and again in 1896-97. The latter victory is perhaps of more interest since it saw the introduction to the side of Bobby Walker, one of Hearts's most famous players. In his early days his lack of pace was remarked upon, but this was to prove irrelevant to his career. His subtle play from the midfield was of the kind

JOHN H. M'LAUGHLIN, SECRETARY,

Was last year's Treasurer of the Celtic Club, which organisation he represents on the League. This year he has been shifted to the onerous position of Secretary, no doubt owing to the tact and ability he displayed last season while performing the duties of Secretary to the League. In the words of one of the League representatives, "Mr. M'Laughlin is one of the best football legislators in Britain." He is also a first-class musician as many of our clubs and social gatherings are aware of to their advantage.

Above: *John McLaughlin of Celtic. An important legislator. He played a vital role in the introduction of both League and professionalism. From* Heads and Tales of the Scottish League *(No. 2).*

Below: *Drawings of an Old Firm game of 1898. Celtic are wearing the stripes — the hooped jerseys were adopted in 1903.*

SATURDAY AT IBROX PARK — RANGERS v CELTIC.

Above: *Rangers team group, c.1900. It includes the players who won all eighteen League fixtures in 1898-99.*
Back row L. to R.: J. Wilson (Trainer), J. Henderson (President), N. Smith, D. Crawford, N. Gibson, M. Dickie, J. Stark, R.G. Neil, J. Robertson, J. Drummond, W. Wilton, (Hon. Match Secretary), A.B. Mackenzie (Committee)
Front row: J. Campbell, J. Graham, J. MacPherson, R.C. Hamilton, F. Speedie, A. Sharp, A. Smith.
Inserts: J. Miller, D. Mitchell, J. Wilkie, T. Hyslop.

Below: *Hearts of 1898-99.*
Back row L. to R.: R. Waugh, J. Arnot, J. Fraser, R. Cheyne, R. Smith, I. Begbie, J. McElfrish, A. Buick, W. Dow, D. Ireland, J. Robertson, G. Walker.
Centre row: H. Rennie, W. Taylor, W. Michael, R. McCartney, G. Hogg, J. Blair, H. Allan, R. Walker.
Front row: J. Dodds, G. Livingstone.

Above: *Clyde v. St. Mirren in 1894.*

Played at Clyde's ground of the time — Barrowfield Park.

which causes other players to flourish. He was also a durable player and it was said that his performance against England in his last season of football (1912-13) showed that time had left his talent unimpaired.

Interest in Scotland-England games had grown greatly since the first, and Celtic, Rangers and Queen's Park all wished to host them. Celtic worked feverishly on their ground and produced by 1896 a modern stadium which could hold 57,000. Having staged the "England game" in 1894 they were rewarded with it again in 1896, 1898 and 1900. Queen's Park, however, were to have the final say in the matter of venue.

Against England things had also been going well. Up to and including the 1900 game Scotland had won 14 victories to England's 9 in 29 games.

On a more pedestrian level, too, the game showed signs of stability. The dispute over the voting rights of clubs in the League which led to eight of them threatening a breakaway in 1900 perhaps catches the modern eye but nothing came of it, and more attention should be paid to what clubs actually did.

December 1898 saw the League somewhat concerned by the fact that Dundee had failed to fulfil a League fixture with Celtic. Rumour said that Dundee were about to become bankrupt and it was determined to try to save the club. The following telegram was sent: "League wish to support you. Send deputation through to Horse Shoe Drury Street 6.30 Wedy. Don't part with players meantime."

At the meeting in that Drury Street bar (which is not unknown to officials of the League in the present day) Mr. Andrew of Dundee confessed himself "sick of the affair". The League, however, agreed to guarantee wages and expenses for the rest of the season and the club was saved. The League had grown strong enough to protect itself.

It is impossible to conclude a discussion of the game in the 19th century without notice of the "England game" of that century's last season. On April 7th 1900 Scotland wore the primrose and pink racing colours of Lord Rosebery, the Honorary President of the S.F.A., for the third time (they first wore them in 1881). The strip was not the only colourful thing about the occasion, for Scotland, thriving on the prompting of Jacky Robertson of Rangers, won 4-1. R.S.McColl of Queen's Park did the bulk of the damage with three first half goals.

Top right: *The Logie Green Final of 1896. Hearts v. Hibs. The goalkeeper is recognisable only by the fact that he is wearing a cap. Distinctive jerseys for keepers were introduced in 1909.*

Bottom right: *The Logie Green Final of 1896. Hearts v. Hibs. The attendance fell around 4,000 short of the 20,000 capacity because of fears concerning the safety of the ground.*

Above: *First Hampden. Opened by Queen's Park in 1873.*

Below: *Second Hampden. Opened by Queen's Park in 1884.*

The Sport of the Nation
1900 – 1914

The early 1900s are marked not by the presence of any great player, nor great game, nor even an outstanding team but by the building of what was the greatest stadium in the world. Queen's Park's inevitable decline (as amateurs in a professional game) should have left them a minor power — the subject of nostalgia rather than of mass interest. They last won the Cup, by defeating Celtic, in 1893 and it was clear that this was a victory against steadily increasing odds. Despite this they took a gamble which was to ensure them a place in the game which no events on the field of play could hope to change. They decided to build Hampden Park.

The desire to build this great edifice sprang, in part, from frustration resulting from their legal position in regard to their home of the late 1880s and 1890s. The first Hampden (named after an adjacent row of terraced housing, which was in turn named after a seventeenth century English parliamentarian) was opened by Queen's Park in October 1873. That piece of land is now occupied by a bowling club and by a section of the Cathcart Circle. It was, indeed, the railway development which forced them to move in 1883. They found a new home of their own, "Second Hampden", and moved into it in October 1884. The land, unfortunately, was leased; that was the start of the trouble and the beginning of a great stadium.

Queen's were loath to develop ground which might be taken back from them and the matter was further complicated by the fact that their landlords (Messrs. Dixon's Ltd.) were themselves sub-tenants of the Corporation. A move to a new location was required.

The need to move coincided with the battle to stage internationals, and the desire to build ambitiously was understandable. Prudent judgement, however, would have seen the idea stifled at birth. The land decided on by the sub-committee of Messrs. Lawrence, Geake, and Sellar (let their names be remembered) occupied 12 acres and was to cost around £10,000. When it was agreed to go ahead with purchase, on April 3rd 1900, Queen's Park had less than £5,000 in the bank. The building of the stands alone required that sum and yet at the A.G.M. of April 1910, less than seven years after Hampden Park was opened, it was announced that all debts had been cleared. Those stands, incidentally, lay along the south side of the ground and there was a gap between them. A centre stand was built in 1906 but its successor and the pavilion which we know today did not appear until 1914.

The ground was opened on October 31st 1903 with a League game against Celtic. Wilson turned home a Logan cross, the home side held on to this lead despite intense pressure and the ground had an auspicious christening. The battle for dominance amongst venues could only conclude with one victor and there has been comparatively little questioning of Hampden's status as national stadium in the years which have followed. In recent times the ground's state of dereliction has brought calls for its renovation rather than pleas for its abandonment. Memories of great games are inseparably tied to the grounds in which they took place; to leave Hampden would be to discard the past.

What became of "Second Hampden"? It was taken over by Third Lanark, re-christened "Cathkin Park", and remained home for that club until their demise in 1967.

Rangers, meanwhile, had begun the new century as they finished the old. They retained the League title in seasons 1900-01 and 1901-02. Rangers found some good players

Above: *Third Hampden.*
The present home of Queen's Park. Here seen around 1904, at which time no centre stand or pavilion existed. A flat which the club rented at 113 Somerville Drive was used as changing rooms.

Top right: *Hampden with the pavilion and centre stand we know today.*

Bottom right: *Hampden Park as it is in 1984. With the reduction of the east terracing and the removal, in 1982, of the north stand, previously situated above the terracing on the right of this photograph, the ground is now at the same level on all sides. This will simplify the task of installing one continuous covering at a future date. Beyond the north-west corner of the ground can be seen Somerville Drive. Photo: George Oliver.*

Below: *Postcard showing Hampden with the centre stand which was erected in 1906.*

International Football Match : Scotland *v.* England, Hampden Park, Glasgow, April 4, 1908

THIRD HAMPDEN PARK.

around this period. In May 1900, for example, they signed [a] centre-half named James Stark. Although he returned t[o] Ibrox from England late on in his career his most importan[t] connection with the club lay in the first period of seven year[s] he spent there. He was one of that rare company o[f] defenders who combine concentration and effectivenes[s] with the kind of relaxed confidence which encourages thos[e] around them to believe the loss of a goal to be an unlikel[y] event. In October of the same year they acquired the brightl[y] named Finlay Speedie from the ranks of junior football an[d] he was to form a natural, and effective, left-wing partnershi[p] with Alec Smith.

The Glasgow Exhibition of 1901 (a form of World's Fair o[f] Commerce and the Arts) inevitably included a footba[ll] tournament in its programme. It was a shortened version o[f] the Scottish Cup (only eight clubs competed) and it wa[s] contested at an extremely unusual venue — Gilmorehil[l.] This was a specially constructed ground situated betwee[n] Kelvingrove Art Gallery and Byres Road, close to Glasgo[w] University. In the Final Rangers survived early pressure b[y] Celtic before goals by Hamilton (2) and Neil gave them a 3-[1] victory.

Left: *James Stark of Rangers*.

Below: *Gilmorehill. Site of the Exhibition Cup Final of 1901. Th[e] stadium itself was a temporary structure and had been removed by th[e] time this photograph was taken.*

GLASGOW FROM THE UNIVERSITY TOWER, LOOKING W.N.W. 18.7.05.

The tragedy of the Ibrox disaster of 1902 meant that Rangers did not have much time to enjoy their possession of the trophy. Rangers had moved into the modern Ibrox in 1899 and the ground was impressive enough to host international football. On April 5th 1902 Scotland played England. Part of the west terracing gave way beneath a large and excited crowd; 25 people died and 587 were to receive compensation for injuries sustained. The terracing was a wooden structure and it is one of history's horrors that a disaster was necessary to show architects that such a flimsily supported construction would not do for a football stadium. The Exhibition Cup was renamed the British League Cup, in a prestigious competition involving Scottish and English clubs which was arranged to raise money to aid the victims and bereaved. It was won by Celtic.

The Cup Final of 1903 is one which, for peculiar reasons, stands out in the history of Rangers. That Final, against Hearts, went to three games and in the last match Rangers, 1-0 ahead, were reduced to ten men when left-back Drummond went off injured. Rangers, for a time, reconciled themselves to dour resistance with Speedie, as so often happens in such cases, proving a useful replacement when he dropped back to cover Drummond's position. Then Stark produced an incisive pass which gave Hamilton a break-away chance; he made no mistake and Rangers had won a 2-0 victory. Remarkable enough, but even more remarkable is the fact that these stirring events might almost have been designed for the future consolation of Rangers fans. They were not to win the Cup again for another 25 years. There is no explanation for this as Rangers had good players and good teams many times over that period.

Initially, their failure may be said to stem from the re-emergence of Celtic. The Celtic team in the 1904 Final had an unfamiliar aspect. It was without the regular centre, Bennett, and Quinn (who was normally a left-winger at the time) came into the team at that position. A double by Speedie put Rangers two ahead before Quinn made his mark by scoring the three goals that gave Celtic victory. The first goal may be taken as summing up Quinn's style. He was put in the clear and his strength made the pursuit by Smith and Drummond ineffective. As a report has it, "Watson could only stand and see the ball being flashed past him into the net".

The rumbustious running and powerful shooting of Jimmy Quinn were to become by-words, yet he was by no means a colossus (only 5ft. 8½ins. in height) and the frequency with which he was to be the subject of injury scares indicates that his opponents were not the only casualties of that style. He was to be the dynamo of the Celtic team, converting dominance into goals with unfailing courage.

The Celtic team from 1904-05 to 1909-10 was the first great team of modern Scottish football. They won six League titles in a row in that period and two Scottish Cups. The styles of its members fitted together as if the whole was entirely the result of planning. If we combined Celtic's League results over that six year period we would have the following figures:

Pl	W	L	D	F	A	Pts
192	136	23	33	444	153	305

A consistent defence included the versatile Alec McNair who commonly turned out at right-back but who was able to play in a variety of positions for the club. He played 583 League games for Celtic (a club record). The half-back line

Above: *Drawing of the Ibrox disaster of 1902. The Scotland v. England match continued since its abandonment might simply have aggravated matters. It is not considered to be an official international.*

Below: *Jimmy Quinn of Celtic.*

'James Quinn, Celtic F. C.'

Above: *Celtic Park in 1900. On the right is the Grant stand. It was named after the director of the club who funded its construction. Its glass front steamed up and obscured the view when a crowd was present. It was never popular.*

Below: *James McMenemy (left) and Alec Bennett, members of the Celtic side of the 1900s. They played together with junior club Rutherglen Glencairn before joining Celtic. Bennett left Celtic for Rangers in 1908.*

of Young, Loney, and Hay had the power, as well as the guile, to take an unremitting grip of any match. The soubriquet of "Sunny Jim", which Young gained, was likely to have been regarded with incredulity by those who played against him. The most famous forward line of the period, however, was the team's glory. Bennett, McMenemy, Quinn, Somers and Hamilton played in a manner which would be recognisable to the modern fan. Their controlled possession play, in which the fine touch of McMenemy and Somers was of particular importance, was deployed with an eye to manoeuvering a position where the ball could usefully be played into space and the power of Quinn unleashed. So fine a unit were they that the presence of the highly talented Bobby Templeton (who had played for some of the biggest clubs in England) in season 1906-07 seemed to be more of a novelty than an addition to the side. Templeton's career casts an interesting sidelight on the financial position of a successful player of the time. He left Celtic to return to Kilmarnock and, in this second spell with the club, earned £4 a week. Nor was that the end of his remuneration, for the club also paid for his keep in the town's commercial hotel. These were highly favourable circumstances when compared with, for example, the wages of a skilled worker in a Glasgow saw mill in 1911. The best paid in that trade earned 36 shillings a week.

More famous than any of the players was the team's manager, Willie Maley. The length of his connection with Celtic seems almost preposterous to anyone accustomed to the frenetic changes of today's game. He was associated with Celtic from December 1887, formally became manager in June 1897 and remained in the position until 1940. One copy of his book *The Story of Celtic* was inscribed by him in the following way: "Willie Maley J.P. Celtic F.C. 1888-1940". He was proud of the social eminence he had attained but prouder still of the central role he had played in the building of a hugely successful football club. There was nothing naive about this for Maley was a shrewd man, happy to use his position with Celtic as the basis of a business career which involved first the ownership of a sports outfitters and later the Bank Restaurant. For that long period, though, the life of Maley and the life of Celtic are indistinguishable.

He had, of course, the resilience which any manager needs to survive. When that first great side of his broke up it did

Above: *Celtic of 1905-06.*
Back row L. to R.: R. Davis (Trainer), R. Campbell, D. McLeod, H. Watson, D. Hamilton, A. McNair, A. Wilson, E. Garry, J. McCourt, D. Adams.

Front row: J. Young, J. Hay, A. Bennett, J. McMenemy, W. Loney, J. Quinn, P. Somers, W. McNair.

Below: *Postcard detailing Celtic's four trophy wins of 1907-08.*

Charity·Cup·Final

CELTIC F.C.
MAKING THE WORLDS RECORD.
GLASGOW CUP, CELTIC 2 RANGERS 1.
SCOTTISH CUP, CELTIC 5, ST MIRREN 1.
SCOTTISH LEAGUE, 4 POINTS
CHARITY CUP, CELTIC 3, Q. PARK. 1.
1908.

NOTHING SUCCEEDS LIKE SUCCESS.

Mr. Secretary Maley: "Leave this to me."

Above: *Cartoon, c. 1900, commenting with distaste upon Celtic's, and Maley's, financial success. Newspapers retained, for many years, a sentimental attachment to the idea of amateurism.*

Above: *The impetuous Bobby Templeton. In 1908, while with Kilmarnock, he entered a lion's den in order to win a wager. In the den, he patted the lion's head and turned its tail. The owners of the menagerie presented him with a gold medal.*

Below: *Dodds and McNair of Celtic. On the eve of the First World War, they were part of the strongest defence in Scottish football. Both were enduring players; McNair won the first of his League-winner's medals in 1906 and the last of his Cup-winner's medals in 1923.*

not take him too long to reorganise and produce further successes. As 1914 approached he had fashioned a different kind of team; one in which Dodds and goalkeeper Shaw combined with the enduring McNair to make sound defence the basis of the team's method. Not that it was a dull team, for it included Patsy Gallagher. Gallagher's greatest fame was to come in the post-war period and consideration of him must be left till later.

It was inevitable that Rangers would react strongly to the dominance of Celtic and the fact that they recovered the kind of supremacy they had held at the beginning of the century was not surprising. A large number of new players were acquired. Lock came from Southampton to bring a high standard of goalkeeping to the club while Hogg, Reid and Bennett (signed from Celtic) brought new menace to the forward line. Later James Paterson was to arrive and take over the influential role once played by Alec Smith. It was a matter of some frustration that Rangers could not, for a time, convert the potential of these players into consistent success. Eventually, though, it arrived and the League was won in season 1910-11 and twice retained. The Rangers team was further strengthened, towards the end of 1913, by the emergence of inside-left Tommy Cairns; a player who added still further drive to a Rangers team already noted for its vigorous, athletic style of play.

Around the same period William Struth gave up his position as Clyde's trainer to take over the same role at Ibrox. From any rational viewpoint, his future in football would not have seemed likely to be great. His experience of the game was scant, for he had been a professional runner in earlier times and his real expertise seemed to be confined to an understanding of the conditioning necessary for success in that sport. In the event, his future career was to confound any such prognostications.

Below: *Celtic's League and Cup-winners of 1913-14.*
Back row L. to R.: W. Maley (Manager), McMaster, Dodds, Shaw, McNair, Johnstone, McColl, Quin (Trainer).
Front row: McAtee, Gallagher, Young, McMenemy, Browning.

GLASGOW CHARITY FINAL.

CHARITY
RANGERS
v
CELTIC

"WHAT, YOU TWO AGAIN!"

Above: *Cartoon from 1904 commenting upon the Old Firm's domination of Scottish Football.*

Above: *The pay-boxes at Hampden alight after the Cup Final riot of 1909. Following this, one correspondent wrote to the* Glasgow Evening Times: *"After Saturday's riot I would suggest the withdrawal of all policemen from football matches, and substitute a regiment of soldiers with fixed bayonets."* Glasgow Herald.

The behaviour of the Old Firm's fans in this period is, sadly, immediately recognisable. In a Scottish Cup-tie of 1905 Celtic fans invaded the pitch and caused the abandonment of the match after seeing Quinn sent off and Rangers assume a 2-0 lead. The tie, of course, was awarded to Rangers. In 1909 a riot followed the second drawn game in the Scottish Cup Final. A few of the players of both sides had stayed on the park at the conclusion, thus giving credence to the idea that there might be extra-time. A riot followed when it became apparent that this would not be forthcoming. Barricades were torn down and a bonfire started. It is even said that whisky was poured on to keep it blazing.

The Old Firm themselves, although highly competitive, bore little sign of association with such barbarous behaviour. Bennett left Celtic for Rangers and Celtic replaced him with Willie Kivlichan — a man who had once been on the books of the Ibrox club. Prior to season 1906-07 Celtic played Rangers in a benefit match for Finlay Speedie. The sequel to that game was, to the modern eye, even more unlikely. Celtic goalkeeper Adams sustained a bad injury in the game and Rangers gave Celtic their reserve keeper, Tom Sinclair, on loan. Of the ten games Sinclair played for Celtic the first nine were shut-outs and a Glasgow Cup medal was won in the tenth. The clubs seem to have lived rather more harmoniously in those days.

As in so many other periods, the other clubs in Scotland tended to be forced by the Old Firm into the role of supporting cast. Happily, though, there were, as always, the exceptions which kept the game from atrophy.

In the early 1900s Hearts and Hibs were of comparable stature to the Glasgow giants. The 1901 Cup Final saw Hearts showing great resilience against a Celtic team which had recovered from a 3-1 deficit to level the match. Many teams would have been broken by this, but Bell scored his second goal of the game and Hearts won 4-3. Hearts had more to offer than just the perceptiveness and control of Bobby Walker. Their centre-forward in that game, Charles Thomson, better known as a centre-half, was reckoned by many to contribute, in his uncompromising manner, almost as much as the inside-forward. Thomson and Walker, it is interesting to note, had the distinction of being the only 'home' Scots in the national team of 1907 which played England.

It was, by this time, becoming increasingly common for clubs to be limited companies. A share issue in 1905 helped Hearts overcome a period of financial difficulty and the measure of security this brought seems to have strengthened the club greatly. They took the Cup again in 1906 and even if Wilson's solitary, scrambled goal in that Final lacked something in drama they could look back on a brave victory at Celtic Park in a previous round.

Celtic had the advantage of playing the Scottish Cup Final of 1902 at their own ground since Ibrox, after the disaster, could not be used. Hibs, though, won a rather grim match when McGeechan scored following a corner from Callaghan. The Hibs team, with its great all-round strength, took the League title the following season, losing only one game on the way. That title was some recompense for their powerful right-winger McCartney, who had missed the Cup triumph because of a broken leg.

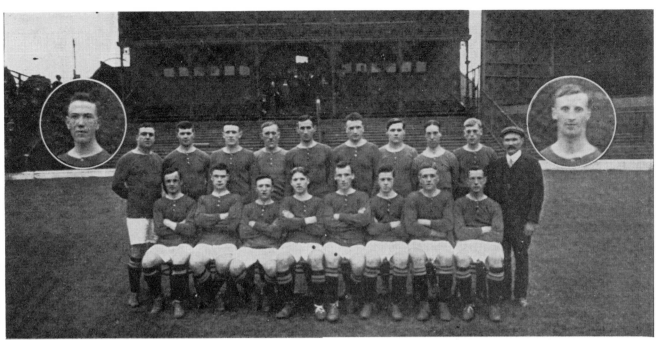

Above: *Rangers, League-winners of 1910-11.*
Inserts L. to R.: R. Brown, A. Richmond
Back row: W. Hogg, D. Taylor, G. Chapman, H. Lock, J. Galt, R.G.
Campbell, J. Hendry, A. Cunningham, A. Gibson, J. Wilson (Trainer).

Front row: A. Bennett, W. Reid, W. Yuill, G. Waddell, J. Gordon, R.
Parker, G. Law, A. Smith.

Below left: Prospectus for Hearts's share issue of 1905. Morton were
the first Scottish football club to become a limited company, in 1896.

Below: Charles Thomson of Hearts.

This Prospectus has been filed with the Registrar of Joint Stock Companies
in accordance with the provisions of the Companies Acts, 1900.

The Subscription List will close on or before 18th April 1905.

The Heart of Midlothian Football Club, Limited.

Incorporated under the Companies Acts, 1862 to 1900

Whereby the liability of each Shareholder is limited to the amount of his Shares.

CAPITAL - - £5000.

Divided into 5000 Shares of £1 each.

458 Shares will be issued as fully paid to the Shareholders of THE HEART OF MID-
LOTHIAN FOOTBALL CLUB, LIMITED (old Company), each Shareholder receiving
One Share.

4542 Shares of £1 each are now offered for Subscription.

Payable 2s. 6d. per Share on Application; 2s. 6d. per Share on Allotment; and the
balance in calls of not more than 5s. per Share, at intervals of not less than
two months.

Directors.

WILLIAM LORIMER, Venetian Blindmaker, 19 Beaverhall Terrace, Edinburgh.
JOHN CAMPBELL, Butcher, 15 Leven Terrace, Edinburgh.
WILLIAM CAMERON PEAT BROWN, Joiner, 23 Marieston Crescent, Edinburgh.
WILLIAM DAVIDSON TELFER, Sanitary Inspector, 22 Merteun Place, Edinburgh.
THOMAS WATERSTON, Dairy Inspector, 30 Duff Street, Edinburgh.
JAMES GALBRAITH ROBERTSON, Tobacconist, 112 Causewayside, Edinburgh.
ROBERT CHEYNE, Butchers' Contractor, 161 Dalry Road, Edinburgh.
JOHN ALEXANDER MURRAY, Spirit Merchant, 10 Polwarth Terrace, Edinburgh.
JAMES GREIG, Joiner 96 Nicolson Street, Edinburgh.

Bankers.

THE NATIONAL BANK OF SCOTLAND LIMITED, 8 Gorgie Road, Edinburgh.

Solicitor.

JAMES G. BRYSON, 50 George Street, Edinburgh.

Auditor.

WILLIAM D. STEWART, C.A. 18 Duke Street, Edinburgh.

Managing Secretary.

W. LINDSAY WAUGH.

Registered Office.

Tynecastle Park, Gorgie Road, Edinburgh.

Third Lanark, too, enjoyed a period of sustained success. They won the League in 1904 and the Scottish Cup in 1905. The League win was extremely unusual since they scarcely had a game on their home ground. The team had not settled into the ground which Queen's Park had recently vacated and most of their fixtures were played at Hampden and other grounds.

Thirds, with Sloan showing great strength and skill in defence, had seemed to have some promising players but it took an audacious signing to turn them into trophy-winners. The player in question was an inside-forward named Hugh Wilson who started his career with Newmilns but had quickly moved on to join Sunderland. In the early 1890s Sunderland took three League titles in four seasons with a team crammed with Scottish players. Wilson was a member of that side. William McGregor, founder of the Football League, lauded them with the description "Team of all Talents." By 1901 Wilson's career seemed over (he was born in 1869) but he was brought back to Third Lanark for a fee of £50. His influence was immediate. In his first game he helped the club to beat Hibs and win the Inter-City League championship. Nor was he simply a figurehead. In the replay of the 1905 Cup Final he scored two of the Thirds goals in a 3-1 win over Rangers.

The goalkeeper for the Cathkin side in those victorious years was James Raeside, an international and a widely respected player. His successor was Jimmy Brownlie, one of the most famous of Scottish keepers. He won nothing of great significance with Third Lanark but his considerable stature allied to reliable judgement brought him one of the rarest of all prizes — a long career as a Scotland keeper. He made his international debut in 1909 and was still playing in the Victory Internationals of 1918-19. He was to manage Dundee United later in his career and more than once injury crises forced him to return as a player. In 1910, when goalkeepers were allowed to handle the ball anywhere in their own half, he and his opposite number, Clem Hampton of Motherwell, both scored from kick-outs in the same match. This event is reckoned by many to have led in 1912 to the change in the laws which confined handling to the penalty area.

Dundee, having overcome their crisis of 1898, found some consistent success in the 1900s. They were runners-up in the League in 1906-07 and 1908-09, and they won the Cup in 1910. If that trophy win is anything to go by the team's forte may well have been endurance. It took them three games to beat Clyde (they were 2-0 down going into the last few minutes in the first game) and their winner in the conclusive match came when their forward John "Sailor" Hunter seized on a defensive error for the winner. The nickname, incidentally, stemmed from his swaying walk. Hunter was to go on to enjoy rather more fame as a Motherwell manager.

The story of provincial achievement in this period is completed by recording Falkirk's Cup victory of 1913. The club had grown in strength in the 1900s and had found one extraordinary player. Jocky Simpson was a highly skilled goal-scoring winger who was selected in 1910 to play in an England International Trial Match. In season 1908-09 he scored 33 goals. Inevitably, he was sold — following that transfer to Blackburn Rovers in 1911 he won 8 full caps with England — but Falkirk, with other such fine players as Croall and Logan, continued to be strong, and their 2-0

Above: *Hugh Wilson of Third Lanark.*

Below: *Jocky Simpson of Falkirk.*

Above: *Dundee. Cup-winners of 1910.*
Back row L. to R.: Dundas, Neal, McEwan, Comrie, Wallace (Manager), Crumley, Dainty, Chaplin, Longair.
Centre row: Hall, Hunter, Langlands, Lee, Macfarlane, Lawson, Fraser.
Front row: Bellamy, McCann.

Below: *Falkirk, Cup-winners of 1913.*
Back row L. to R.: J. Drummond, A.F. Carmichael, W. Nicol, R. Waugh, C. Chapman.
Second row: G. Drummond, M. Gibbons, J.Morrison, A. Stewart, T. Logan, J. Donaldson, J. McMillan, J. Rattray, A. Brown.
Centre row: R.C. Liddell, S. McDonald, J. Robertson, R. Orrock, R. Terris, R. Hamilton.
Front row: J. McNaught, J. Croal.

Top: *Orion play Victoria United in Aberdeen before 1903. The venue is probably Cattofield.*

Centre: *Aberdeen F.C. 1889–90. Aberdeen F.C., Orion F.C. and Victoria United amalgamated to form the modern team of the same name in 1903.*

Below: *Orion F.C. 1901-02.*

victory over Raith Rovers won them that season's Scottish Cup.

The history of football involves more than just the winning of trophies and current events make it important to note the birth of two teams: Aberdeen and Dundee Hibernian (later to undergo a change of name).

Aberdeen were created in 1903 by the amalgamation of three teams (Orion, Victoria United and Aberdeen F.C.). They finished seventh in the Second Division of 1905 and even though the First Division was about to be expanded from fourteen to sixteen teams they should not, on the face of it, have stood any chance of promotion. In those days the votes of the First Division teams determined such questions and Aberdeen found themselves in the top division in time for season 1905-6. This move may have lacked something in fairness but the League were right to recognise the need to encourage football in a significant, if distant, area of the country.

Aberdeen were quick to give evidence of their potential. The terracing of their Pittodrie ground was extended and they built a new pavilion. On the playing front, they signed Willie Lennie (previously of Queen's Park, Dundee, Rangers and Fulham). Nor was he a veteran returning to fritter away his last few years with a provincial side. He was 23 when he signed for the club and was to go on to become the first Aberdeen player to be capped.

It is the good fortune of clubs who are at an early stage in their development that they are able to take risks which others, with more to lose, could not. Donald Colman was born in 1878 and went on to have a football career which seemed, for a long time, to be doomed to mediocrity. He played in the junior ranks until he was 27 before embarking on a disastrous two years with Motherwell which ended in a free transfer. Aberdeen took a chance on him and were rewarded prodigiously. He was an immediate success, forming a celebrated full-back partnership with the hardy Jock Hume. The balance and intelligence of his play even brought

him caps. The last was won against Ireland in 1913 and he was still playing for Aberdeen in 1920.

Colman was later to be manager of the club and is generally credited with inventing the dug-out. His reasons for doing so are far more interesting than the invention itself. He wished to study the ball control of the players from what he deemed to be the best possible view. Perhaps his own career had imbued him with a sense that players might be helped to develop, for he was an enthusiastic coach who encouraged those under him both to think about the game and to improve their skills.

Early in 1909 the Irish community in Dundee formed a team called Dundee Hibernian and took over the ground of the defunct Dundee Wanderers. At first the club seemed set to grow strong. Their first match attracted over 5,000 people and they quickly entered the Scottish League.

The club, however, never seemed to recover from the war and left the League in 1922 after a dreadful season. Local businessmen saved them and after much argument in Dundee the name Dundee United was adopted as part of an attempt to draw a broader support. They were re-admitted to the League in 1923.

On the international scene prior to the First World War England were showing disturbing signs of parity with Scotland, winning four games and losing four between 1902 and 1914. The international setting still proved to be the stage for some important Scottish players. There was, for example, Alec Raisbeck who played first for Hibs and then Liverpool before returning to Partick Thistle. Unusually for a centre-half he was an exciting player who used his considerable pace to intercept the ball and switch the flow of the game.

The Scottish League continued during the war but in such altered circumstances it is difficult to evaluate the games of the time. In any case, football seems decidely insignificant against such a backdrop. The entire Hearts first team enlisted and many of them were killed in the conflict.

Top: *England v. Scotland at Newcastle in 1907. Scotland are wearing the Rosebery colours. On this occasion they drew.*

Centre: *Hearts on tour to Copenhagen in 1914.*

Below: *Unveiling of the Hearts war memorial in 1922. The monument also now bears the names of those killed in the Second World War.*

Top left: *Alex Jackson. Here seen shortly after his £8,500 transfer from Huddersfield to Chelsea in 1930.* Glasgow Herald.

Top right: *Alex James.* Glasgow Herald.

Above: *Jack Harkness (Queen's Park and Hearts).* Glasgow Herald.

Right: *Jack Harkness. In Harkness's playing days teams remained on the pitch at half-time and took refreshments there.* Glasgow Herald.

Between the Wars
1918 – 1939

Below: *Programme for the "Wembley Wizards" match.*

The minutes ticked away and the game moved on into a prolonged injury-time but still the referee did not blow the final whistle. Yet there seemed no reason for the delay since all tension and doubt concerning the result had long since vanished. Then the ball found its way into Jack Harkness's hands, the whistle blew, and Scotland had won the 'England game' at Wembley in 1928 by five goals to one. The referee was a Scot, the visiting team in those days being entitled to a referee of the same nationality, and he had delayed until Harkness, with whom he was friendly, had the ball in his possession. In the dressing room the laces were cut and the ball deflated and stored safely in the keeper's bag. That precious relic of the "Wembley Wizards" match now holds a position of honour in the S.F.A.'s offices.

That game, one of the principal glories in the history of our sport, was a showcase for some of Scotland's most famous players but it also serves as a reminder of the enduring, fascinating oddity of football, for it might all have ended so differently.

The season had been a miserable one for both Scotland and England. The Home International Championship had been quickly won by Wales. England had lost both to that country and to Ireland. Scotland and England were fighting to avoid the dreaded imaginary trophy, the wooden spoon. Team selection on both sides owed much to chance and fortune. The English captain, Bishop, for example, became ill during the night before the game and was unable to play. The Scotland team, for its part, was the product of some decidedly strange decisions. Eight 'Anglos' were picked and some very celebrated 'home' Scots were passed over. It seemed almost lunacy to prefer Gallacher to McGrory at centre-forward when the former was still serving a two month suspension when the team was announced.

Everyone now knows that Scotland, at the instigation of their captain, McMullan of Manchester City, "prayed for rain" and were rewarded with the tricky conditions suited to their diminutive, clever forwards. In reality, though, the advantage of such a surface would not have been immediately obvious to the casual observer. The young Harkness had come on to the field, been overcome by nerves and formed the opinion that the flagpoles above the ground were revolving. He was forced to hold on to the post to regain his composure and retain his balance. His cause could not have been helped when in the opening minutes England's first real attack tore the Scotland defence open and ended with the ball rebounding from the post.

It is only at this point that the triumph begins. McMullan took possession of the ball and it was eventually played out to Morton on the left. He chipped the ball over and Jackson headed in. Twice more in the game Morton was to cross and Alex Jackson to score; these goals allied to two by Alex James gave Scotland their five. It was a dazzling display of inventive, technically assured attacking, but Scotland had stars throughout their team. The English attack led by the menacing Dixie Dean applied much pressure but the Scotland defence rallied around the towering figure of Bradshaw and held firm.

The following year saw an equally historic win by the Scotland team although the circumstances were markedly different. In the first half Jackson had fallen and dislocated his elbow. Soon he was lying in the Victoria Infirmary, his senses dulled by the chloroform which had been used while the elbow was re-set. Suddenly he sat up and announced

J.Harkness

J.Crapnell J.Nibloe

J.Buchanan D.Meiklejohn J.M'Mullan

T.Muirhead A.James

A.Jackson H.Gallacher A.Morton

SCOTTISH INTERNATIONAL TEAM 1929

Above: *Postcard of the Scotland team of 1929. The team shown is the one which, with the exception of Tommy Muirhead of Rangers, played against England. Muirhead had to withdraw from the side after injuring his nose in the Cup Final. His place was taken by Alex Cheyne — the scorer of the game's only goal.*

"That's the winner for Scotland". So, indeed, it was. He had heard the distinctive roar through the drugged haze.

Scotland had been reduced to ten men by Jackson's injury, for there were no substitutes in those days. They had concluded that they should play the ball, when possible, into the corners of the England half and so relieve the pressure for as long as could be contrived. The tactics worked well and Scotland took satisfaction from the fact that the game was scoreless as it drew near its close. Then, with two minutes to go, Scotland won a corner. In the absence of Jackson, Alex Cheyne of Aberdeen took it. It had seemed that the English defence would clear it but, unaccountably, it was left to float into the net for the game's only goal.

The Scotland team in those years included some of the most famous names in all of football but it also bore sad testimony to the financial pull of England. In a perceptive move Aberdeen had bought Alex Jackson and his brother Walter. Alex Jackson, having already spent a brief, exotic period with Bethlehem Star in America only stayed long enough to confirm the effectiveness of his roving, free-ranging style of play and he soon signed for Huddersfield.

The magnificent Alex James had started his career with Raith Rovers and was part of that club's most celebrated forward line of Bell, Miller, Jennings, James and Archibald.

Popular wisdom said they were worth £50,000, but, sadly, financial considerations meant that this fantasy estimate was to be checked against reality. Within a short space of time they were all sold, and collectively earned the club less than £10,000. So, Scotland was denied the regular sight of James's mature play. He had a wonderful ability to switch from holding the ball in midfield with his shuffling, close control to releasing a long, raking pass to his winger. The sight of Bastin of Arsenal chasing such a James pass was to become one of the most celebrated in the history of English football. James also ensured that he himself would be regarded as an unforgettable sight since the inordinate bagginess of the shorts he favoured seemed more appropriate to a comedian in the Music Hall than to a slick footballer.

Perhaps James's life lost something in colour when he left Raith. One incident in that club's history of the time suggests that a player's life with them would lack nothing in excitement. In 1923 they went on tour to the Canary Islands and found themselves shipwrecked when their ship, *Highland Loch*, ran aground near the Spanish village of Villa Garcia. There were no casualties. The father of Jimmy Mathieson, a player who had been chosen for the tour at the last minute, had bragged endlessly to his workmates about his son's success. News of the maritime escapade effectively silenced him. The Raith Rovers players must have had strong nerves for they eventually won their three tour matches.

The business of touring abroad started, as so often, with Queen's Park. They planned to tour to Denmark in 1879 and although it is unclear if they actually did so they certainly played there in 1898. By the 1920s it would perhaps have seemed 'chicken' to visit anywhere so adjacent. In 1923 Raith Rovers were joined on the ship home by Third Lanark who had been playing in Argentina. Thirds, with the aid of some guest players, had billed themselves as "Pick of Scotland". It may be that they received some intimation of the future strength of South American football for they lost two of their eight games.

In 1922 Celtic made their third tour of Czechoslovakia (the previous ones being in 1904 and 1911) and were beaten by Slavia — a team coached by Johnny Madden, a former player of theirs. Madden was not the only Scot to influence football in that country. Jacky Robertson, one of the stars of the 'Rosebery game' of 1900 also coached there. The fiscally minded would have been consoled for poor performances by the fact that Celtic had been guaranteed £1,200 for their three games on tour. Rangers, in 1928 and 1930, visited America and played on both occasions in New York against Fall River. Scotland went on tour for the first time in 1929 and played internationals in Norway, Germany and the Netherlands. The following year they played in Paris and beat France 2-0 before embarking on a leisurely week of sight-seeing. The only problem of the tour arose when their trainer, Mattha Gemmell of Clyde, experienced difficulty in procuring "thick black" tobacco.

The war, of course, had brought difficult times to Scottish Football. From season 1915-16 to 1920-21 only one national League was in operation. After the war some of the clubs who were not in that Division broke away and formed the Central League. The renegades found they had considerable success on their hands and their bargaining position was a strong one. When the two bodies were reconciled and a Second Division re-established, for season 1921-22, the

Above: *The Raith Rovers party in a hotel on their 1923 tour.*
Standing: Brown.
Seated L. to R.: Ritchie, Bell, Alex James, Morris, Cowie and a visitor.
The photograph belongs to Alec Cowie.

Below: *Alex Cheyne's corner kick beats goalkeeper Hacking for Scotland's late winner against England, 1929. It has sometimes been said that Hacking was impeded by a Scottish player standing on his foot. The photograph provides no support for this excuse.*

Above and below: *Celtic in Czechoslovakia in 1922. The players (below) are: Front row L. to R.; McFarlane, Cringan, Gallagher, Cassidy, McAtee. Second row: Gilchrist and W. McStay. Third row: McNair and McLean. Fourth row: McMaster and goalkeeper Shaw. Willie Maley can be seen between Cringan and Gallagher.*

League were forced to concede a system of automatic promotion and relegation. The status of clubs would, from then on, be entirely dependent on playing performance. Queen's Park, at the end of the season, lost their First Division status for the first time.

In general, the normal fare of Scottish football was of a high standard between the wars despite that constant loss of talent to England. There was, for example, the sight of Alan Morton, outside-left in the "Wembley Wizards", playing. Morton began his career with Queen's Park and although born in 1893 did not join Rangers till 1920. That delay seems to have been of service to him for he was able to bear with apparent ease the burden of being the key player in the great Rangers team of the time.

He is remembered for his ability to make his crosses bend and dip with cruel accuracy. Such an attribute was rare in Morton's time because of the nature of the ball in use. Without the coating of its modern successor, it grew heavier and heavier in wet conditions. The winger was accordingly required to make constant re-adjustments to his game. The kind of 'strike' which would produce a delicate chip early on would produce only an apparent 'mishit' in the latter stages.

Many players, however, have had a fine touch and Morton had additional qualities of even greater significance. Some clue to his character is given by the fact that though he played outside-left he was naturally right-footed. Much of his skill was the result of sheer hard work. The fact that he was a dapper figure who was taken on to the Board at Ibrox as soon as he retired should blind no-one to the raw determination he possessed. He was not called the "Wee Blue Devil" for nothing. Once he had satisfied himself that his opponent could be beaten he would give the unfortunate in question no respite. It is frequently said of ball-players that they "flattered to deceive" but that comment could rarely, if ever, have been applied to Morton.

Top: *Davie Meiklejohn leads out Rangers. Torry Gillick and Dougie Gray behind. Glasgow Herald.*

Centre: *Rangers of season 1927-28, in which they finally broke their Cup hoodoo.*
Back row L. to R.: R. McPhail, W. Hair, H. Shaw, W. Moyies, A. Cunningham, R. Hamilton.
Centre row: D. Meiklejohn, T. Lockie, J. Marshall, R. Ireland, T. Craig, J. Docherty, A. Archibald, J. Hamilton, J. Fleming, J. Simpson, D. Gray, J. Osborne, T. Hamilton.
Front row: W. McCandless, G. McMillan, T. Muirhead, W. Chalmers, A. Morton.

Below: *Alan Morton in action with Queen's Park, pre 1920.*

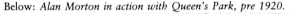

Above: *Kilmarnock. Cup-winners of 1920.*
Back row L. to R.: J McAdam, H Wilson, H Spence (Secretary), R Russell, R Thomson.
Second back row: W Cunningham, P. Carrick, T Hamilton, T. Blair,

D. Gibson, J. McWhinnie, A. Gibson.
Centre row: J. Morrison, J. McNaught, M. Smith, J. Smith, W. Culley, M. McPhail, C. Smith.
Front row: A. Mackie, M. Shortt, R. Neave, T. Bagan.

For all that the years between the wars belong to Rangers, it has to be noted that they struggled for a time to beat their Cup jinx. Those years saw the birth of Kilmarnock's reputation as dangerous opponents in the Cup (as recently as 1978 they knocked out Celtic). In the 1920 Cup Final they played Albion Rovers who had beaten Rangers in the semi-final. The game and the score swung wildly between the teams but Kilmarnock, driven on by their veteran centre-half Shortt, scored a late goal through J.R.Smith and won by three goals to two.

Even once Rangers had taken that Cup the sense of a jinx must still have remained for they lost to Kilmarnock in the 1929 Final. It appeared at the outset that the Ayrshire team would be brushed aside but the magnificent goalkeeping of Sam Clemie kept them in the game. The breakthrough seemed to have arrived when Rangers won a penalty in the seventeenth minute but Clemie saved Craig's kick. Despite moments of worry, Kilmarnock took heart and went on to win 2-0.

The occasion was further soured for Rangers by the sending off of one of their players — Jock Buchanan. Until Roy Aitken of Celtic, in 1984, he was the only man to have been sent off in a Scottish Cup Final.

Kilmarnock, though, were to discover how unrewarding a business it is to play outsiders in Cup Finals. Celtic and Rangers were beaten on the way in the 1938 tournament and Kilmarnock were faced with East Fife (a 2nd Division team) in the Final. The first match was drawn and East Fife

were 2-1 down in the replay. McLeod equalised for them and Miller and McKerrell scored to give them victory in extra-time. In the first game of the Final, Herd, scorer of four goals in the Cup that season, had been injured. The crisis this provoked was resolved in a unique manner. In those days a player could not be Cup-tied and East Fife manager Dave McLean was able to sign John Harvey on loan from Hearts Harvey's playing career with East Fife only lasted 120 minutes but it brought him a Cup-winner's medal. His next meeting with his 'team mates' was for an official photograph. East Fife are the only Second Division team to have won the Scottish Cup and they also possess the same distinction in the League Cup.

Partick Thistle took the Cup in 1921 despite severe injury problems. They were without Willie Hamilton and Jimmy McMullan (who was later to captain the "Wembley Wizards") and were forced to press into service the less than fit Jimmy McMenemy who had joined Thistle after his long and glorious career with Celtic. McMenemy won his seventh Cup-winner's medal. His pass freed Salisbury, an eccentric winger in the great Thistle tradition, and Blair scored from his cross. With a fine sense of timing Thistle were to wait for fifty years to take their second major trophy by handing out a considerable beating to the other half of the Old Firm.

Rangers took their revenge by beating Thistle in the Final of 1930, but the Jags had other moments of joy in the years up until 1930. In 1927 their centre-forward Sandy Hair

Above: *Partick Thistle. Cup-winners of 1921.*
Back row L. to R.: A. Lister (Trainer), W. Hamilton, T. Creighton, K. Campbell, J. McMenemy, M. Wilson, J. Bowie, W. Borthwick.

Front row: D. Johnston, J. Kinloch, J. Harris, W. Bulloch, J. McMullan, R. McFarlane.
Seated: J. Blair, W. Salisbury. Glasgow Herald.

scored five against Rangers in the Glasgow Charity Cup Final, which Thistle won 6-3 after extra-time. This achievement showed Hair's utter impartiality for in 1923-24, his first season of senior football, he scored the two goals at Celtic Park which gave Thistle their first ever League victory over the Parkhead side.

In 1922 it was Morton's turn to take the Cup. A goal by Jimmy Gourlay from a free-kick gave them the win. Morton seem to have had little confidence in their ability to win the Cup for they had arranged to go direct from Hampden to play West Hartlepool on the Easter Monday. They had even made special arrangements for the south-bound train to stop for them at Mount Florida. The citizens of Greenock had no chance to acclaim the heroes until the following Wednesday. The first public reception for the team took place in West Hartlepool when the local team, impressed by the newly-gained stature of their opponents, arranged for a pipe band to meet them at the station.

In 1924 it took Airdrie seven hours of football to rid themselves of Ayr United (four matches in all, two with extra-time) in the fourth round. In the Final, two headers by inside-right Russell gave them a rather more comfortable victory over Hibs. Airdrie's side that day included Hughie Gallacher and Bob McPhail.

St. Mirren won the Cup in 1926 by defeating Celtic. That surprisingly clear-cut 2-0 victory, film of which was shown at La Scala, Paisley at 7pm on the same day, might be said to have brought the club their second major trophy. After the First World War the Scottish clubs played a competition for the Victory Cup. This was intended to be an equivalent to the Scottish Cup (which had not re-started) but the fact that clubs were in some cases without the services of certain players who were still conscripted makes the competition difficult to assess. St. Mirren themselves were without seven players and had to borrow McKenna and Page from Rangers for the Final. In that game, against Hearts at Celtic Park, one of their goals was scored by a man named Hodges who was officially a Birmingham player at the time. The fact that no presentation was made after the match because the Cup had not yet been made might suggest that the competition was based on an original idea by Lewis Carroll. The winning of it was, however, a praiseworthy achievement and the fact that 60,000 attended the Final suggests that there was no shortage of people to take it seriously.

Perhaps St. Mirren had something of a penchant for acquiring strange trophies for they took another in 1922. In that year, Barcelona decided to inaugurate their splendid new ground with a game between St. Mirren and Notts. County. It had taken the Paisley team eleven days to reach Spain but they must have recovered fully for they beat the English team 2-1 after extra-time.

It seems likely that the finest team to be seen outside of the

Above: *East Fife. Cup-winners of 1938.*
Back row L. to R.: D. Russell, W. Laird, R. Tait, J. Milton, J. Harvey, A. Herd.
Front row: T. Adams, D. Millar, R. McCartney, J. Sneddon, E. McLeod, D. McKerrell.

Below: *Airdrie. Cup-winners of 1924.*
Back row L. to R.: G. Carroll (Trainer), W. Neil, R. McPhail, J. MacDougall, J. Ewart, T. Preston, D. Gordon, J. Allan, J. Murdoch, W. Reid (asst. Trainer).
Front row: J. Sommerville, J. Reid, W. Russell, H. Gallacher, G. McQueen, A. Dick, R. Bennie, J. Howieson.

Above: *McCrae scores St. Mirren's first in the 1926 Cup Final.*

Below: *St. Mirren. Cup-winners of 1926.*
Back row L. to R.: T. Hart, G. Riddell, J. Fleming, T. Craig, J. Cochrane (Secretary and Manager).
Centre row: W. Walker, T. Morrison, A. Findlay, J. Bradford, W. Newbiggin, W. McDonald, A. Reid (Trainer).
Front row: M. Morgan, A. Gebbie, D. McCrae, J. Hall (Chairman), W. Summers, J. Howieson, J. Thomson.

Old Firm in the inter-war years was the Motherwell side of the late '20s and '30s. They were managed by John "Sailor" Hunter and the fact that he finally brought them success says much for his powers of endurance. He became manager of Motherwell in 1911 but found, for many years, that his skills in recruiting good young players to the club were largely wasted since the lure of England could not be resisted by a team of Motherwell's financial status. Finally, Hunter managed to assemble a team from the ranks of the Juniors and keep it together. Even then bad luck seemed to dog him. His team led Celtic by 2-0 with eight minutes of the 1931 Cup Final remaining. In the last minute they were still ahead by two goals to one but their centre-half Allan Craig, in an attempt to cut off a cross aimed at Jimmy McGrory, scored an own goal. Inevitably, Celtic won the replay. Some have said that the Celtic centre would have scored if Craig had not touched it but McGrory was to say in later years that he reckoned the ball would have eluded him.

Happily, Motherwell, in season 1931-32, set a record for the time by scoring 119 League goals as they triumphantly took the League title. Only the hardest of hearts could fail to rejoice at this reward for dogged persistence. The effectiveness of the team's attack was largely the product of three men — centre-forward Willie McFadyen, inside-left George Stevenson and outside-left Bobby Ferrier. On the way to that title McFadyen scored 52 League goals and in doing so created a record which still stands. It seems almost needless to say that he was a natural finisher who tended to conserve his energy until such time as the ball was in his opponents' penalty area. The left-wing partnership of Stevenson and Ferrier has become almost legendary in the game. The goal-scoring record of Ferrier is astonishing and that fact speaks volumes for the creative abilities of Stevenson who built so many of the moves. Wingers of the time habitually hugged the touchline but Ferrier was a glorious exception. In 626 League matches for Motherwell he scored 256 goals. However, his Scottish parents had carelessly allowed him to be born in England, so that the national side, under the rules of the time, could not include the Ferrier-Stevenson partnership.

Top left: *Allan Craig of Motherwell. Scorer of an o.g. in the 1931 Cup Final.*
Bottom left: *George Stevenson of Motherwell.* Glasgow Herald.
Below: *Bobby Ferrier of Motherwell.* Glasgow Herald.

The whole business of scoring goals had been made rather easier by the change, in 1925, of the offside law. Previous to this it had required the presence of three members of the opposition between him and the goal for the attacker to be onside. In season 1924-25, 1,178 goals were scored in First Division football; in 1925-26, after the change, 1,337. In 1924-25 Dundee United had won the Second Division title and scored 58 goals in the process. The following season Dunfermline won it and scored 109 goals.

The Old Firm sides nevertheless dominated the period and their teams of the '20s and '30s contained some very famous names. There was, for example, the Irishman, Patsy Gallagher of Celtic. At the time of his debut for Celtic in 1911 Gallagher was 5ft 3in and weighed 7st. Eventually he grew to be 5ft 5in. He was a determined player despite his size and had no qualms about retaliating against larger opponents who had mistreated him. He took care of himself off the park as well and made sure that he earned considerably more than his team-mates. Once when chosen to play for Ireland against England at Windsor Park, Gallagher refused to change into his strip until he had discussed the question of

Left: Willie McFadyen of Motherwell, scorer of 52 league goals in season 1931-32.

Below: Dundee United. Second Division champions in 1931.
Back row L. to R.: Taylor, Penson, Milne, McCallum, Gardner, Qusklay.
Front row: Logie, Bain, Bennett, Kay, Cuthill.

Above: *Patsy Gallagher in acrobatic action. Quinn (right) looks on.*

Right: *Theatre postcard. Patsy Gallagher is seated between the two entertainers in the front row.*

Below: *Jimmy McGrory scores for Celtic against Partick Thistle in 1933.*

payment with the treasurer. That gentleman, conscious of the effect Gallagher's absence would have on the huge crowd, acceded to his financial demands. It is said that Gallagher received what was for the time the highest fee ever paid to an international.

This slight, almost deformed man played with a brilliance of a somewhat alien variety. He had splendid ball control and the ability to hit the telling pass when the opportunity arrived but he did not look like an orthodox player. There was a lithe, determined, almost gymnastic quality about him which had, in the best sense, something of the circus about it. His famous goal in the 1925 Cup Final was reckoned by many to sum him up. Celtic were one down to Dundee, a goal scored by a former player of theirs called McLean, when Gallagher took the ball on half-way. Several times he appeared to have been upended by an opponent only for him to recover his balance and continue on his way. He seemed to have beaten the keeper when he was again knocked to the ground. This time, he somersaulted into the net with the ball wedged between his feet.

Goals of so strange a nature do more than change the score; they win matches. It was no surprise when McGrory scored the winner.

McGrory was perhaps the other outstanding Celtic player of the inter-war years. His astounding figures of 397 goals in 378 League games with Celtic bear testimony to the magnitude of his contribution to the club. For sentimental reasons he was sometimes regarded as a second Jimmy Quinn but his style was different. His characteristic goal would come with a powerful header from a cross (the crosses often being provided by Paddy Connolly on the right).

On one occasion against Hearts he hurled himself at a cross and would have collided with the post except that the Hearts keeper Harkness (of the "Wembley Wizards" team) pushed him wide of it. The incident tells us much about his concentration on 'attacking' the cross, as well as his courage, for he told Harkness later that he had been completely unaware of the nearness of the post.

His Scotland career was limited but, paradoxically, successful. He won seven caps and, in the two games he played against England (1931 and 1933), scored three goals. It says much for the combative, clever Hughie Gallacher (of many clubs) that he overcame his lack of height to develop a quality of play good enough to keep McGrory out of the Scotland team. McGrory's second goal in the 1933 game was supplied from a pass by the powerful Bob McPhail and that Old Firm combination produced a roar which has become legendary. The 1930s were comparatively good times for Scotland against England. They won at Hampden in '31, '33, '35 and '37. Their Wembley experience of the time was less joyous but the match of 1936 was worth remembering.

Scotland were losing by one goal to nil when Crum of Celtic was brought down and Scotland were awarded a penalty. It was taken by Tommy Walker of Hearts, who was only 20 at the time. The ball was twice blown off the spot, but Walker's nerve held firm and he eventually scored. He had not performed particularly well that day but his skilled play was a major factor in Scotland's brilliant 3-1 victory at Hampden the following year. Walker played for a good Hearts side which won nothing of consequence but his international feats stand as a reminder of the high quality of a man who is, unusually, remembered not only for the quality of his play but also for his sunny nature on the park.

LINDSAY & HARTE, SCOTTISH ENTERTAINERS,
In their Great Football Sketch, CELTIC v. RANGERS.

WEST-END PLAYHOUSE, GLASGOW.

"Lindsay & Harte prove themselves the most popular comedy artistes seen at this House for some time."

"Their skit on a girl's first visit to a football match is one of the best mirth provokers seen in Glasgow."
The Evening Times, January 6th.

O'OR BEST MAN.

[Photo by The Evening Times, Glasgow.

Above: *Scottish Cup Final 1937. Willie Cooper of Aberdeen and Jimmy McGrory of Celtic pursue the ball. A crowd of 147,365 looks on.*

Below: *John Thomson in action in the game in which he was fatally injured.* Glasgow Herald.

149,415 spectators had watched the 'England game' of 1937 (a record for an international in Europe) and the following week 147,365 saw Celtic beat Aberdeen in the Cup Final (a record for a club match in Europe). On that latter occasion, it is reckoned that there were 20,000 locked outside the ground.

The following year saw Celtic win the Empire Exhibition Cup. The Cup, involving top Scottish and English teams, took place at Ibrox and was part of the festivities of the Exhibition itself, which was centred on Bellahouston Park. Celtic beat Everton in the Final. Their forward-line of the time was considered by some to be, in its fine blend, comparable to the club's forward-line in the 1900s. Delaney, Macdonald, Crum, Divers, Murphy played in a fluid, inter-changing manner which was revolutionary in that period. Delaney is a particularly interesting figure for he was to add to his Scottish Cup success Cup-winner's medals from England (Manchester United) and Ireland (Derry City).

Sadly, Celtic's history in the 1930s is marked by tragedy. On September 5th 1931 their goalkeeper, John Thomson, died in a collision as he dived at the feet of the Rangers centre Sam English. He was an excellent keeper and that fact added, understandably if illogically, to the pathos of the accident. There were 30,000 at his funeral at Cardenden. Perhaps, though, a certain ghoulish fascination with the Old Firm background to the accident has played its part in the creation of the legend. Certainly, the club's international midfield star, Peter Scarff, who died after long illness at the age of 25 in 1933, is remembered by comparatively few.

Above: *The John Thomson tragedy. The moment of collision, September 5th 1931.* Glasgow Herald.

Below: *A somewhat flummoxed Bob McPhail accepts a pre-match gift from the opposing captain during Rangers's tour of Germany in 1933.*

Between the wars, Rangers were undoubtedly Scotland's greatest side. In that period they won the Cup six times and the League fifteen times. Between season 1922-23 and season 1930-31 they won the League in eight of the nine campaigns.

The most significant factor in all this was Rangers' ability to introduce new players to the side while maintaining the highest of standards. So, for example, the sound goalkeeper Tom Hamilton was replaced by one of the greatest of all goalkeepers, Jerry Dawson. Dawson, indeed, was given much of the credit for frustrating England in the early stages of that famous Scotland victory of 1937. Rangers replaced Jimmy Gordon with Billy McCandless at left-back in 1920 and scarcely noticed the change, although Gordon, who could both tackle powerfully and use the ball constructively, is widely thought of as one of the club's greatest full-backs.

Rangers were wise, too, in their buying of players. The long-serving Tommy Cairns was replaced by Bob McPhail who brought not only a great capacity for hard work to the inside-left position but also showed a considerable aptitude for goalscoring. His ability to make the kind of runs which allowed him to meet Alan Morton's crosses made him a particular menace for goalkeepers. McPhail won seven Cup-winner's medals — one with Airdrie and six with Rangers. He is still the club's record goalscorer with 233 goals in 354 League matches.

There was, also, Davie Meiklejohn, who is often spoken of as Scotland's greatest ever captain. He was so complete a player that Rangers fans could indulge themselves in arguments over whether he should be Scotland's right-half or centre-half. He was more than just a skilled player however. His performance in dragging Rangers, in one game, from 3-0 down to a 4-3 victory over Celtic was a subject of awe in the football world.

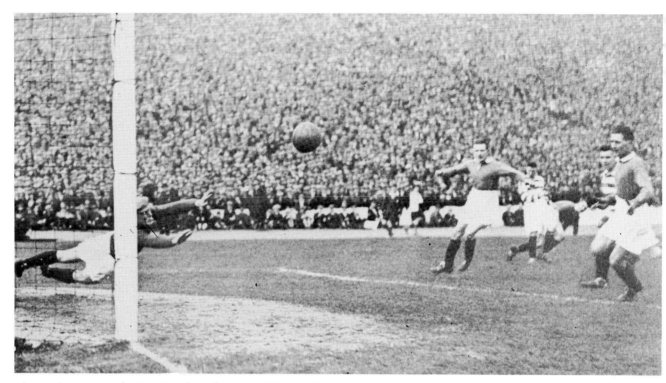

Above: *The great save by Tom Hamilton of Rangers which kept the score at 0-0 in the 1928 Cup Final.*

Right: *William Struth of Rangers with a portrait presented to him at the City Chambers (Glasgow) in 1953. The portrait now hangs in the Ibrox trophy room.* Glasgow Herald.

Below: *McStay concedes the penalty whch gave Rangers the lead in the 1928 Cup Final.*

It is probable that Rangers only became entirely happy when they at last took the Scottish Cup in 1928. They broke their run of misfortune in a way their supporters would have regarded as ideal — they beat Celtic. For all that, it was a nerve-wracking game. At 0-0 it had taken a magnificent save by Hamilton to prevent their opponents taking the lead. Then, in the second-half, Willie McStay of Celtic handled to prevent a Fleming shot from going in. Meiklejohn took the penalty and, forcing from his mind thoughts of the historic position he found himself in, scored. It was as if Rangers knew they had broken that long curse and were revelling in the fact as they went on to score three more goals through McPhail and Archibald (2).

Throughout this period, Rangers were managed by William Struth. He inherited the post when William Wilton was drowned in a boating accident in 1920 and he remained in charge until his retirement in 1954.

There was an immense aura of discipline about Struth. He himself was impeccably dressed — he had a wardrobe full of suits in his office — and required that his players displayed the same kind of neatness. Jack Harkness recalls that he was once at the main entrance of Ibrox chatting to a very famous Rangers player who was standing casually with his hands in his pockets. Struth came out from the entrance, saw the player and, without warning, punched him powerfully in the ribs.

Struth's attitude perhaps stemmed from his memories of the earlier difficulties of his life. He was determined both to protect Rangers and, by doing so, maintain his own hard-won status. As a young man he had been a professional runner and had once entered himself in a race at Porthcawl. He had to win for he had no money and, understandably, had no wish to be trapped there. Having spent the night sleeping on the ground in a tent he went to the track and found he was to be given a handicap that made it impossible for him to win. Struth, pretending he was not running in the race, sauntered 20 yards from the mark he had been given, and eventually won the event. He had won, taken the money and left the town before officials at the meeting, having discovered the truth, could catch up with him. It was a story that Struth often told. Although he treated the incident only as a humorous anecdote, it is likely that he found the desperation he must have felt hard to forget.

In any case, his record proves that he was an extremely gifted manager, for success on that level could not have been achieved merely by the ability to frighten those beneath him. He was able to make players share in his determination to bring the club success.

Above: *Hughie Gallacher.*

Below: *Willie Maley (left) and John "Sailor" Hunter. Managers of respectively, Celtic and Motherwell. Seen here in the 1930s.*

Colour Plates

The colour plates on pages 58–64 (with the exception of Celtic player Jim Craig's medals from the 1960s) feature players, clubs, grounds, medals, ornamental buttons, and a brake club banner, from the first years of this century, c. 1900 to 1912.

The colour plates on pages 65–68 feature some memorable moments and achievements from the past decade.

Drawing by Tom Malone.

1870's

1890's

1910's

1930's

1950's

1970's

CELTIC

GROUND~CELTIC PARK, PARKHEAD, GLASGOW.

The Bould Bhoys!

CELTIC

"COME AWAY CELTS"

W & A.K.Johnston. Limited, Edinburgh & London.~ Series 181/2

Above: Two Celtic postcards. The Celtic player above wears the striped jersey which was the club's normal strip until 1903. The Celtic player on the right wears the jersey with green and white hoops, which has remained the club strip since then. Collection: Jack Murray.

Left: Medals won by Jim Craig in the 1960s. *Back row L. to R.:* Glasgow Cup, League Cup, League Championship. *Front row:* Scottish Cup, European Cup, badge awarded by Celtic to members of the 1966-67 "Grand Slam" squad.

58

Above: *Jacky Robertson. The greatest Scottish wing-half at the turn of the century. He masterminded Scotland's 4-1 win over England at Celtic Park in 1900. He joined Rangers in 1899 after spells with Everton and Southampton and later worked as a coach in Czechoslovakia. Collection: Jack Murray. Top right: Rangers postcard from the early 1900s. Collection: Jack Murray. Below: Ibrox in the 1900s. Collection: Jack Murray.*

Above: *Partick Thistle Brake Club Banner, 1911*

Below: *Partick Thistle postcard. They moved in 1908 from their home at Meadowside, Partick to Firhill, where they play today. The present ground was only completed in 1909, and home matches were played at Ibrox in the intervening season.* Collection: Jack Murray

Above: *R.S. McColl. Fondly remembered for scoring a hat-trick against England in 1900. Queen's Park were his first club and he returned to them at the end of his career. Afterwards, he established a chain of sweet shops.* Collection: Jack Murray.

Above: *David Wilson, the Queen's Park inside-forward, played from the 1890s to the early 1900s, winning one cap. Died in the 1st World War. He was the scorer of the first ever goal at modern Hampden on October 31st 1903 against Celtic.* Collection: Jack Murray.

Below: *The current Hampden. Opened in 1903 with a League match against Celtic, won by a single goal from Wilson. The twin towers seen here never existed, there was no permanent centre stand or pavilion until 1914.* Collection: Jack Murray.

Above left: *Third Lanark postcard. Founded in 1872, the club went out of business in 1967. They won their first major trophy by taking the Scottish Cup in 1889. Collection: Jack Murray.*

Above: *Medal for Scotland v. England game of 1912. Awarded to Jimmy Brownlie of Third Lanark.*

Below: *Medals won by T.P. Sloan of Third Lanark. Left: League Championship medal of 1903-04. Right: Scottish Cup medal of 1905.*

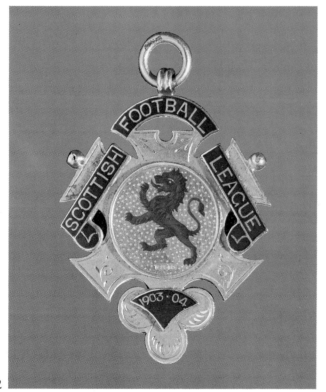

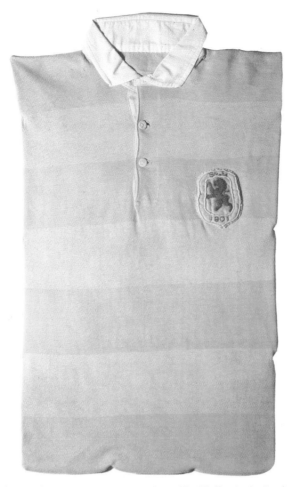

Above: *The Rosebery jersey worn by Bobby Walker in the Scotland v. England match, 1901. The Rosebery strip was also worn in games against England in 1881, '82, 1900, '05, '06, '07, '08, and against France in 1949.*

Top right: *Bobby Walker postcard. He is here pictured wearing the Rosebery colours. The most celebrated occasion on which Scotland wore Lord Rosebery's colours was their 4-1 victory over England in 1900. Collection: J. Hutchinson.*

Below: *Hamilton Crescent. This Glasgow cricket ground was the scene of the first international, Scotland and England drawing 0-0 on November 30th 1872. The Scottish team was entirely composed of Queen's Park members. Collection: Jack Murray.*

DUNDEE

GROUND DENS PARK. DUNDEE.

Good old Dundee!

Above: *Dundee postcard. The club was founded in 1893.* Collection: Jack Murray.

Above: *Ornamental buttons c. 1900.*

Below: *Dundee of 1909-10. In that season they won the Scottish Cup.* Collection: Jack Murray.

DUNDEE. F.C.

Photo by Agnew & Son, Glasgow

Back Row : W. WALLACE (*Sec. & Manager*), J. CHAPLIN, J. FRASER, A. LEE, B. NEAL, R. CRUMLEY, J. DUNDAS (*Linesman*)
Front Row : J. BELLAMY, G. LANGLANDS, A. MACFARLANE, H. DAINTY, A. MENZIES, J. LAWSON, W. LONGAIR (*Trainer*)

Above: *David Hay's shot goes just over the bar, Scotland v. Brazil, World Cup Finals 1974. The game ended in a 0-0 draw. Colorsport.*

Below: *Dalglish in action, Scotland v. Yugoslavia, World Cup Finals 1974. Scotland's last game in the tournament, since the draw (1-1) was not sufficient to see them qualify for the later stages. Colorsport.*

Above: *Lorimer scores, Scotland v. Zaire, World Cup Finals 1974. Scotland's first goal in that year's tournament.* Colorsport.

Below: *Joe Jordan in action, Scotland v. Holland, World Cup Finals 1978. The eventual margin of victory (3-2) was not great enough and Scotland went out of the tournament on goal difference.* Colorsport.

Above: *Narey scores, Scotland v. Brazil, World Cup Finals 1982. With this goal Scotland took a shock, early lead.* Colorsport.

Below: *Eder's stunning goal, Scotland v. Brazil, World Cup Finals 1982. Alan Rough can only watch the ball sail into the net. Brazil's third in a 4-1 victory.* Colorsport.

Above: *John Hewitt heads the winning goal, Aberdeen v. Real Madrid, European Cup Winners' Cup Final, Gothenburg, May 11th 1983.* Sportapics.

Below: *Dundee United with the Premier League trophy they won in season 1982-83. Paul Hegarty is being chaired by (L. to R.) Iain Phillip, Paul Sturrock, Hamish McAlpine, David Narey, Richard Gough, David Dodds, Derek Stark, Maurice Malpas. Front row: Ralph Milne, John Reilly, Billy Kirkwood, John Holt, Eamon Bannon.* Sportapics.

A Place in the World
1945 – 1965

At the end of the Second World War football was quick to recover and confirm its importance in the mind of the nation. In 1945 Rangers and Queen's Park even played friendlies in Germany against British Army teams despite the obvious difficulties in arranging matches in such circumstances. Queen's Park found little reward for such missionary zeal. Fog prevented their return to Glasgow and their second team was forced to fulfill a League fixture against Queen of the South.

An equally intriguing and doubtless more glamorous, fixture took place at Ibrox in November 1945. The touring Russian team, Moscow Dynamo, had caused great excitement. Public curiosity may have been disappointed by the fact that they appeared to be normal human beings, but a certain vestigial air of mystery still hung around them. They had impressed many with their thoughtful football as they fulfilled their first three fixtures on tour without defeat. There had indeed seemed little likelihood of their losing in any of those matches. Their final match was at Ibrox and Rangers impressed the 90,000 who attended by recovering from 2-0 down to equalise and even threaten victory. Playing Moscow Dynamo should not be regarded as similar to playing a normal match. Prior to the game they had registered a rather frivolous protest about the eligibility of some of the Rangers team, and it was also found, at one point in the match itself, that some confusion regarding substitutes had arisen. Moscow Dynamo briefly had twelve men on the park.

Rangers were almost always a fine team in the 20 years that followed the end of the war and it was, again, the Russian connection that gave them one of their best chances to demonstrate the fact. In the summer of 1962 Rangers toured Russia. They won their first two games and drew with the Russian champions, Dynamo Kiev, in the third.

Below: *Rangers v. Moscow Dynamo. Ibrox 1945.* Glasgow Herald.

These performances gained them a huge reputation in Russia and the crowds which saw them grew from 20,000 in the first match to 60,000 in the last. Their fine blend of poise, typified by the "wee prime minister" Ian McMillan, and pace excited home crowds accustomed to a rather more cautious style of play.

In footballing terms, the story of "the Scot abroad" tends towards either farce or tragedy but in this case Rangers greatly boosted their country's reputation and it was appropriate that the team was met by thousands of enthusiastic fans on its return to Renfrew Airport.

Above: Moscow Dynamo players with expensive cameras. Ibrox 1945. Glasgow Herald.

Below Rugby Park during the Second World War, when it was requsitioned by the Army.

Football had tenaciously survived the war itself. Indeed, games with England continued as regularly as ever even if the proceeds of a match might go to such an unusual cause as Mrs. Churchill's "Aid to Russia" fund and the programme might offer some rather phlegmatic instructions about the course of action to be adopted in the event of an air raid.

On the domestic front the game survived in a somewhat fractured form with trophies such as the Regional League and the Southern League being played for. The war produced some particularly striking disruptions in the normal order of things. Kilmarnock found their ground requisitioned and used as a site for fuel tanks. More glamorously, Morton were able to play Stanley Matthews and Tommy Lawton, who were stationed in the area. Their team also included Billy Steel. St. Mirren, however, managed to beat a team containing those three great players in the Summer Cup of 1943. The trophy for one competition, the Southern League Cup, was recalled by the S.F.A. at the end of the war and used as the Victory Cup. Rangers took it by beating Hibernian 3-1 at Hampden in June of 1946.

The years which followed were ones of great success for Rangers. The institution of the League Cup gave clubs a new target: the treble. Rangers became the first to achieve it in season 1948-49. It was the period of the club's "Iron Curtain" team. The term, borrowed from the burgeoning "Cold War" rhetoric of the time, was used to refer to the massive solidity of the Rangers defence. The club had the joy and misfortune of possessing two magnificent centre-halfs,

Members of Rangers's "Iron Curtain" defence.
Left: *Jock "Tiger" Shaw*. Glasgow Herald.
Above: *George Young*. Glasgow Herald.
Below: *Willie Woodburn*. Glasgow Herald.

Above: *Willie Waddell scores for Rangers against Queen of the South.*
Glasgow Herald.

Below: *Scot Symon, manager of Rangers.* Glasgow Herald.

Willie Woodburn and George Young, and the latter was, accordingly, often played out of position. Both of them stood in the Meiklejohn tradition and Young's force of character earned him the position of Scotland captain on the record number of 48 occasions. Sadly, Woodburn's determination was allied to an extremely bad temper and his disciplinary record eventually led to his being banned *sine die* by the S.F.A. It is interesting to note that he was sent off only five times in his career — a figure surpassed by several players since. Woodburn and Young were daunting enough in themselves but the presence in the team of such unforgiving tacklers as Sammy Cox and Jock "Tiger" Shaw made a game against Rangers an unappealing prospect for any forward.

It is easy to underestimate the creative abilities of that Rangers side, however. The common, over-simplified story suggests that all Rangers' goals came from a cross by Willie Waddell and a header by Willie Thornton. A lot of them did come that way but, accomplished though Waddell and Thornton were in such moves, it has to be said that such a tactic can only work if a team has the skill to disrupt a defence which enters the game already aware of the exact source of danger in the opposition.

The facts confirm, in any case, that Waddell could do rather more than simply cross the ball. He scored 143 goals in 558 first team games. His goal scoring with the club began when, as a seventeen year old making his first team debut, he scored the only goal of the game against Arsenal. Rangers have generally had the good fortune to have splendid players whose abilities have not stopped them from playing a team game. Waddell was such a player and his aggressive wing play, skilful and entertaining though it was, was never employed for his own entertainment.

Inevitably, old age brought something of a decline in William Struth's powers and when he retired in April 1954 a rebuilding job awaited the new incumbent, Scot Symon. Symon had been a gifted all-rounder. As well as being a fine midfield player with Dundee, Portsmouth, and Rangers, he is also the only man to have played for Scotland at football and cricket. The Hearts player of the '70s, Donald Ford, played only one-day cricket for his country. Symon took 5 for 33 off 18 overs in the first innings of Scotland's two-day match with Australia in 1938 and his victims included the celebrated batsmen, Fingleton and Barnes. Before returning to Ibrox in 1954, Symon had gained valuable experience with East Fife, whom he had taken to League Cup success, and Preston North End. He was dignified, shrewd and taciturn — a mixture which made him an appropriate choice for the manager's chair at the club. It is said that a reporter once phoned him to ask about weather conditions at Ibrox since it seemed there was the possibility of a fixture there being cancelled. "Is it foggy at Ibrox?" he asked. A long pause followed while Symon considered a reply. "No comment", he finally offered.

Symon worked patiently to build Rangers another good team. It was in the early 1960s that the success of his work began to be seen. There were, as always with the club, the solid and uncompromising defenders. This time they were called Bobby Shearer (otherwise known as "Captain Cutlass") and Eric Caldow. They were, however, part of a team which included some wonderfully skilled players. Ian McMillan was brought from Airdrie in 1958 to add the qualities of generalship which fashion a team out of a collection of players. Up front there were durable and skilled players like Alex Scott and Davie Wilson. Better still for the Rangers fans there was the sight of John Greig and Willie Henderson beginning to make their mark. The complete contrast in the styles of those two suggests how much success Rangers were having in producing a variety of good players. Greig allied a prodigious will to win with a simple but effective style and was to provide much of the possession which gave the side a platform for its attacks. The rather myopic Henderson was the archetype of the Scottish winger — small, tricky and possessing an endearing exuberance.

The star of the team, though, was Jim Baxter. Rangers signed him from Raith Rovers in 1960 and he brought an intriguingly individual style of play to a club who were, perhaps understandably, wary of such a thing. The fact that he had, as a teenager, briefly given up the game was a clear indication that he was unconventional. On the park he played with a languid elegance which precluded such unseemly activities as tackling, but his influence was enormous. Even the simplest of passes, when made by Baxter, had a distinguished look about it and many teams were to find themselves demoralised by the effortless superiority he displayed. Celtic, notably, went through a long period of being overawed by his talismanic power. It is easy to say that he might have achieved more or had a longer career as a player if he had been more dedicated but the fact remains that he entertained mightily.

Under Symon Rangers became the first Scottish team to reach the Final of a major European competition, losing to Fiorentina over two legs in the first ever Cup Winners' Cup Final of 1961.

That visit to Germany in 1945 had gone rather badly for Rangers, for the British Army of the Rhine team, composed of some very good English players, beat them 6-1. One writer was moved to advise the S.F.A. on how this debacle might be avenged:

> So if you want to shine again,
> And bring back Scottish Pride,
> See Mr. Travers right away,
> And he'll send out the Clyde.

That might seem like a counsel of desperation but the 1950s were to provide evidence that Clyde were a good side for they twice won the Scottish Cup.

Their Final against Celtic in 1955 was the first to be televised and Clyde had something extraordinary in store for the occasion. With three minutes left Celtic led 1-0 against a Clyde side which had, understandably, shown many signs of stagefright. Then Archie Robertson took a corner on the right and the inswinging ball curled over the fingers of Bonnar and Clyde had levelled the match. Robertson confessed that he had had no intention of playing the ball so near the goals but Clyde took heart from that strike and were a transformed side in the replay. In that game their lively outside-left Tommy Ring scored the game's only goal and so brought the Cup to Shawfield for the second time. They had first won it by beating Motherwell 4-0 in 1939.

Things went rather awry for Paddy Travers's Clyde thereafter. Before their next appearance in the Cup Final in 1958 they had been relegated in season 1955-56 and promoted in season 1956-57. There were only four players remaining from 1955. One of the newcomers was Johnny Coyle, a prolific goalscorer, and a deflected shot by him gave Clyde a 1-0 win over Hibs in the 1958 Final. Appropriately,

Above: *John Greig*. Glasgow Herald.

Below: *Willie Henderson*. Glasgow Herald.

Above: *Archie Robertson's equaliser against Celtic in the Scottish Cup Final of 1955*. Glasgow Herald.

Top right: *Jim Baxter*. Glasgow Herald.

Bottom right: *Tommy Younger of Hibs*. Glasgow Herald.

Below: *Tommy Ring 'nutmegs' an opponent in a Scotland v. Army match*. Glasgow Herald.

the Cup was later brought by two of the Clyde players to the house of Mattha Gemmell who had been too ill to attend the Final. He had served the club from 1898 until 1945, mostly in the capacity of trainer.

As Rangers faltered a little in Struth's last few years as manager their position was usurped by Hibs.

The war-time period had seen Hibs lay the foundations for those successful years in the late '40s and early '50s. Some indication that things might well be going to plan came when they beat the usually dominant Rangers team of that period 8-1 in September 1941. Willie McCartney, who had managed Hearts for many years, had taken over the running of the club in 1936 and, by the close of the war, had a team in which Gordon Smith was an established player and Lawrie Reilly was beginning to make his mark. Captained by the international full-back Davie Shaw, they took the League title in season 1947-48. The key game, in all likelihood, was their 1-0 victory over Rangers late in January 1948, for only two points separated the teams at the end of the season. Sadly, McCartney did not live to see the success he had planned, for he died in January 1948.

In the early 50s, under the management of Hugh Shaw, Hibs were the best team in Scotland if not in Britain. Their most celebrated forward-line of Smith, Johnstone, Reilly, Turnbull, and Ormond began to make regular appearances, although injuries and other factors meant that they did not play together quite as often as is sometimes imagined.

The League was won in 1950-51 and retained the following season. On the first occasion the margin of victory was a crushing ten points. Hibs had, of course, more than just a celebrated forward-line in their favour. The versatility of Bobby Combe, who played in five different positions in season 1951-52, gave the club the range of possibilities in team selection which is required to cope with a bruising, tiring season. In goals, by this time, they had the sound Tommy Younger. He was, in the early 1950s, doing his National Service in Dusseldorf but Hibs, realising the value of a sound goalkeeper, made arrangements to have him flown back to Britain every Friday by British European Airways. Perhaps the regularity with which Younger was

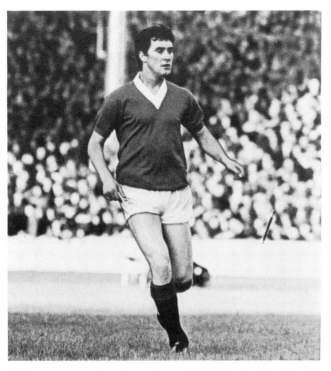

able to get a weekend pass is explained by the fact that he was serving with the Royal Scots.

The European Cup was the brainchild of Gabriel Hanot, editor of the French sports paper, *L'Equipe* which invited Hibs to be Scotland's representatives in the first European Cup (1955-56). This was partly a recognition of Hibs's excellence in the early '50s and partly a reward to their chairman Harry Swan for his advocacy of the idea of European football. Once U.E.F.A. took control of the tournament, thus legitimising it, the S.F.A. approved Hibs's entry despite the fact that Aberdeen were the League champions of 1954-55. This kind of behaviour by the S.F.A., understandable though it was, would not (and, indeed, could not) take place today. The European Cup had not, at that time, earned the prestige it was soon to enjoy. Chelsea, the English champions, eventually decided not to take part. In a sixteeen team competition Hibs advanced impressively to the semi-final stage before losing to Reims. The European Cup tournament as a whole attracted huge public interest and immediately assumed a position of great importance in the game.

Having acknowledged the worth of the entire Hibs team, it is hard not to return to the "Famous Five" for there is no doubt that their names have gathered a potency which guarantees them a permanent place in the game's history. It is right that they should be remembered as a unit, for the perfect way in which their styles complemented one another was perhaps the most startling thing about them.

Bobby Johnstone had the kind of cocky outlook which any player requires if he is to be a regular goalscorer. On a more practical level, his powerful shooting was of more than passing significance to his success. It was not enough, however, simply to plan to deny Johnstone opportunities, for Turnbull and Ormond possessed a comparable weight of shot. Turnbull's industry was much admired but the longevity of his career and the fact that he was able to play, in a slightly deeper role, until well into his thirties shows that he was astute as well as strong.

Any successful winger requires courage since the position inevitably involves direct and repeated conflict with the opposition's full-back. Ormond possessed that quality in great abundance. His committed style meant that he was frequently injured and in his career he overcame three broken legs and, even more serious, ruptured ligaments.

At outside-right there was Gordon Smith. In his Hibs days it might have been reasonable to describe him as a winger but his fine control and accurate passing meant that he was the kind of player who could expect a long career since his effectiveness did not particularly rest on pace or physical strength. He was to go on to play for Hearts and Dundee, with astonishing success, in the role of midfield playmaker.

The centre-forward was Lawrie Reilly. Reilly joined Hibs from school and was to play for no other club. He was quick and highly intelligent and the fact that he is, with 38 caps, Hibs's most successful international gives much force to the argument that he is the club's greatest player. His success as a striker was largely based on the sharpness with which he could size up a situation and produce the appropriate kind of shot. This quality of alertness suited him perfectly to the demands of international football and it also played its part in the making of one of the most famous of all goals in Scotland-England games. In the last minute of the 1953 Wembley game Scotland were losing to England by two goals to one. Then a chance fell to Reilly, who had scored that single Scottish goal. Refusing to be distracted by the figure of Alf Ramsey (later to manage England), who was closing in on him, he lifted the ball neatly over the keeper. It is pleasant to note that Reilly had the endearing habit of scoring goals against England — six in all.

Hibs's "Famous Five"

Top left: *Eddie Turnbull*. Glasgow Herald.
Above: *Bobby Johnstone*. Glasgow Herald.
Left: *Gordon Smith*. Glasgow Herald.
Top right: *Lawrie Reilly*. Evening News (Edinburgh)
Right: *Willie Ormond*. Glasgow Herald.
Far right: *Lawrie Reilly*. Glasgow Herald.

Above: *Lawrie Reilly flicks the ball over the keeper to equalise in the last minute of the 1953 game against England at Wembley. Alf Ramsey looks on.* Glasgow Herald.

Top right: *Baxter sends Banks the wrong way from the spot to score his first goal against England at Wembley in 1963.* Syndication International.

Bottom right: *Baxter, out of picture, scores his second goal at Wembley in 1963. Law and St. John admire.* Syndication International.

On the whole, Scotland's record against England from the '40s to the early '60s makes distressing reading. There are, however, some potent, if unusual, moments to consider. In 1949 one of the rarest of Wembley occurrences for a Scottish goalkeeper gave the side a 3-1 victory — Jimmy Cowan, of Morton, played a blinder. Two years later Scotland again won at Wembley, with Reilly scoring one of their three goals, but, in the years that followed, the ground became something of a graveyard for Scottish hopes. In 1955 Scotland lost 7-2 and in 1961 England even managed to better that performance in winning 9-3. Perhaps it was to be expected that matters would improve for Scotland only when everything seemed against them. In 1963 the Rangers full-back, and Scotland captain, Eric Caldow broke his leg after six minutes. There being no substitutes at that time Scotland were reduced to ten men. They went on to win 2-1, with Baxter of Rangers scoring both goals and outside-left Davie Wilson (also of Rangers) taking up Caldow's position as if it were a matter of no concern for him to play in such a role.

Scotland's performance against England at Hampden also gave cause for depression. Our win there in 1962 was the first in official internationals for 25 years.

Below: *Scottish fans in London, 1953.* Glasgow Herald.

Further serious doubts about the standing of Scottish football in the period emerge when we consider the sorry tale of Scotland's involvement in the World Cup. Things had been changing in world football and the point was driven home by the performance of the Hungarian team of the 1950s. In 1953 they became the first continental side to beat England at Wembley and did so by the crushing margin of 6-3. The manner in which they won was even more of an admonition than the scoreline. The fluidity of their play and the supreme ease which the whole team displayed when in possession of the ball were a massive rebuke to British football, which had, on the whole, stolidly retained its outdated approach to the game. It was the Hungarians who finally killed the nonsensical idea that players should be deprived of the ball in training in order that they might be hungry for it on Saturday. The play of Bozsik, Hidegkuti, Puskas and company left British fans wishing that the home-grown product could display such ease on the ball.

Scotland, to their credit, provided the Hungarians with an interesting match at Hampden in December 1954, but finally lost by 4-2. Any thought that Scotland was in a healthier state, in a footballing sense, than our neighbours may, however, be discounted. The World Cup which had taken place earlier that year had made Scotland's defects manifest. In the Finals in Switzerland they had lost both their games. In the light of their performance against Uruguay their 1-0 defeat in their first game, against Austria, seems almost worthy of praise. Uruguay won 7-0 and it was clear that world football had left Scotland far behind; an English critic commented that the Scottish defenders stood around like Highland cattle.

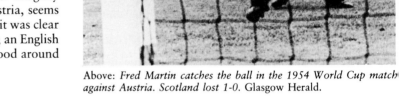

Above: *Fred Martin catches the ball in the 1954 World Cup match against Austria. Scotland lost 1-0. Glasgow Herald.*

Below: *The Scotland party leaves for the 1954 World Cup. Glasgow Herald.*

Prior to that match the Scotland manager, Andy Beattie, had announced that he intended to resign. It is hard to know whether to disapprove or to congratulate him on his prescience. Beattie, it should be said, cannot be much blamed for Scotland's performance, for he was only one member of a selection committee and, in any case, only thirteen players had been taken to Switzerland.

Scotland's first point in a World Cup Finals came in 1958 when a goal by Jimmy Murray (of Hearts) gave them a draw against Yugoslavia in Sweden. Compared to the Switzerland experience the defeats which followed against Paraguay and France, by 3-2 and 2-1 respectively, were something of an improvement. It was to be 1974 before Scotland again qualified for the final stages but at least we had, by then, become more worthy opponents.

Where international football is concerned, the 1940s saw one of the most singular of careers. On October 1st 1949 the imposing figure of Henry Morris marked his debut for Scotland by scoring three times in an 8-2 victory in Belfast. Such precocity seems to have counted for little for he was never selected again.

His career with East Fife brought a measure of fulfilment. In season 1947-48 he was at centre-forward as his club mirrored their unique Scottish Cup achievement of 1938 by becoming the first (and, so far, only) Second Division team to win the League Cup — the feat being achieved with a Duncan hat trick in a 4-1 win over Falkirk in a replay. In the 1949-50 Final East Fife, having acquired First Division status in the interim, jealously guarded that distinction by beating Second Division Dunfermline 3-0, Morris scoring one of the goals. Morris was also a consistent scorer, notching 41 of East Fife's 103 in their promotion-winning season of 1948-49. The solidity of the side was the product of the formidable half-back line of Philp, Findlay, and

Aitken. The right-half and left-half were miners.

In season 1953-54 East Fife, by this time without Morris, took their third League Cup when a late goal by Frank Christie killed off a Partick Thistle fight-back and produced a 3-2 win.

The denial of entry to the European Cup for Aberdeen was not the only time they had found themselves plagued by ill-luck. They won the League Cup on the first occasion it was played (season 1945-46), but the competition was a truncated one and the victory is now regarded as unofficial. The following season saw their first indisputable success. The Aberdeen manager David Halliday had carefully gathered an extremely sound team but it seemed in the first minute of the 1947 Scottish Cup Final against Hibs that they would continue to be dogged by misfortune. Their goalkeeper, George Johnstone, fumbled a pass-back and Cuthbertson scored for Hibs. Despite a missed penalty late in the game Aberdeen still managed to record a win by two goals to one. The winner came in forty-two minutes when their South African right-winger Stan Williams impudently shot home from the byeline as everyone awaited the cross.

Aberdeen rebuilt, and took the League title in season 1954-55. That team had some entertaining players — men like Harry Yorston and Graham Leggat — but the fact that they lost only 26 goals in the League that season suggests that their defence had much to do with their success. Goalkeeper Fred Martin was an unusual figure for he had been an inside-forward with the club until he left on National Service. In the Army he was forced to play in goals and did so well that Crystal Palace wrote to Aberdeen to ask if they might play him. Halliday was, of course, astonished but when Martin returned to the club in 1949 he was given his chance as goalkeeper.

Below: Aberdeen. League-winners of 1954-55.
Back row L. to R.: J. Hather, A. Glen, W. Smith, J. O'Neil, R. Morrison, F. Martin, R. Wishart, J. Allister, J. Wallace, D. Caldwell, G. Leggat.

Front row: J. Robbie, W. Mitchell, J. Brown, R. Paterson, P. Buckley, J. Mitchell, A. Young, H. Yorston, G. Hamilton, C. Forbes, D. Halliday (Manager).

Above: *Stan Williams's winning goal in the 1947 Cup Final.*

Below: *Aberdeen return home after the 1947 Cup win.*

Above: *Ian St. John scores for Motherwell against Airdrie.* Glasgow Herald.

Life, however, continued to be a struggle for those outside the Old Firm. Motherwell, for example, unearthed an extremely effective goal-scorer in Ian St. John but although he entered the Scottish record books by scoring a hat-trick in two and a half minutes against Hibs, he left for Liverpool shortly before his 23rd birthday. Worse still, brilliant players like Denis Law began to go directly to England and were never seen in domestic football. Law was to become the greatest international scorer for Scotland, 30 in 55 games, but his breathtaking reactions and exhilarating finishing were generally enjoyed by "foreigners".

Hearts, too, suffered from that trend when they lost the accomplished and powerful Dave Mackay to Tottenham Hotspur in 1959. By that time, though, Hearts had at last become winners again. Bitterness had expressed itself as mockery in Edinburgh and Hearts's failures were useful source material for all comedians. Under Tommy Walker's management, though, they took the Scottish Cup, by beating Celtic, in 1956 — 50 years after they had last won the League or Scottish Cup. The League Cup had been taken in season 1954-55 with a 4-2 victory over Motherwell — 3 of the Hearts' goals coming from Willie Bauld. Hearts hit their peak when they took the League title by a crushing 13 point margin from Rangers in season 1957-58.

Walker had added steel to the side. As well as Mackay and Cumming in midfield there was, in defence, the determination of full-back Bobby Parker. The traditional Hearts virtues of silky, intelligent play did not suffer in the process.

In addition to the almost disdainful attacking skills of Alex Young, who was later to go to Everton, there was the "Terrible Trio". As with the "Famous Five" their success had much to do with blending. Bauld supplied aerial strength, Wardhaugh terrific pace. Conn, although highly skilled, was prepared to do the thankless and necessary work, graft being alien to Bauld's style. In that League-winning season of 1957-58 Wardhaugh scored 28 of Hearts's record tally of 132 League goals. Hearts again won the League in season 1959-60, with the veteran Gordon Smith in their side, by pipping Kilmarnock, but the Ayrshire club was to have its full measure of revenge.

Possible success followed by dispiriting failure had become a way of life for Kilmarnock. Since their 1929 Cup victory they had, before season 1964-65, been runners-up in that competition four times and four times in the League. Willie Waddell, the club's manager, announced that he would retire at the end of the season. His nicely balanced team responded by at last winning a trophy.

In goal there was the young Bobby Ferguson, who was later to play for Scotland, and on the right wing the tricky play and beautiful crossing of another future international — the teenager Tommy McLean. There was experience, too, in the form of players like Davie Sneddon, who had played with Preston North End, and Frank Beattie. It seemed that the title might elude them again when they found themselves playing Hearts at Tynecastle in the last game of the season, needing a 2-0 win to prevent the Edinburgh side from taking the title. The likelihood of their winning the trophy seemed to paralyse Hearts and goals from Davie Sneddon and Brian McIlroy produced the desired result. The title was won on a goal average, the margin being .04.

Dundee were also to have notable success in the period. They won the League Cup in seasons 1951-52 and 1952-53. Their star player was Billy Steel. He had been on Morton's books when he played, and scored, in the Great Britain v. The Rest of Europe match in 1947. He then went to England for a record fee of £15,000. In an ambitious move the inside-left was brought back by Dundee for £23,500 in 1950. He combined an energetic style of play with the perception of an extremely cunning strategist. Although he was an individualist whose temperament could create difficulties in a team, he nonetheless played a vital part in bringing those League Cups to Dundee.

An unfancied Dundee team, managed by Bob Shankly, took the League title in season 1961-62. They had Gordon Smith playing for them and although not far from his fortieth birthday he had the intelligence to adapt his style to his physical condition, and played good accurate passes to his forwards from a deep position on the right. Forward of him were Alan Cousin and that uncannily skilled header of a ball, Alan Gilzean. As late as the early '70s, while with Tottenham, Gilzean's flicks were helping Martin Chivers to gain the kind of reputation which brought him England caps. In defence there was the commanding figure of Ian Ure.

Dundee's quality became apparent when they beat Cologne 8-1 in the European Cup the following season. The return leg was something of a bloodbath. Goalkeeper Bert Slater had to go off injured and, for a time, Dundee had to play midfield man Andy Penman in goals. Slater, finding the pain of watching worse than the injury, returned to the field. Dundee went on to reach the semi-finals of the competition.

Hearts's "Terrible Trio"

Left: *Willie Bauld*. Glasgow Herald.
Above: *Jimmy Wardhaugh*. Glasgow Herald.
Below: *Alfie Conn leaps for a corner. Beattie of Celtic intercepts.*
Evening News (Edinburgh).

Above: *Dave Sneddon scores the first in Kilmarnock's vital League win at Tynecastle in 1965*. Daily Record.

Below: *Brian McIlroy scores Kilmarnock's second goal at Tynecastle in 1965. This goal brought Kilmarnock the title on goal average*. Daily Record.

Left: *Billy Steel (white shirt) being challenged by McLure of Raith Rovers. Glasgow Herald.*

Below: *Dundee celebrating in the Muirton stand after the League win over St. Johnstone which brought them the title, 1962.*

Above: *Stand-in goalkeeper Andy Penman is beaten. Cologne v. Dundee, 1962. The injured Slater, having fought off an ambulance crew, returned to the pitch and replaced Penman a few minutes later. At the conclusion of the game it took the intervention of Scottish soldiers, stationed in Germany and attending the game, to see the players through an incensed crowd to the safety of the dressing rooms.*

Above: *Alan Gilzean scores against Kilmarnock, 1964.* Glasgow Herald.

Freshness was brought to the Cup in the fifties by the victories of Motherwell, Falkirk and Saint Mirren.

The Motherwell of the early fifties were overshadowed by their classic predecessors of the thirties, but despite that the later team enjoyed a distinctive success. It was they who gave Motherwell their first Scottish Cup win. They played Dundee in the 1952 Final and it was not expected that a large crowd would be attracted. In the event, the attendance was 136,000 and the late arrival of a train meant that many Dundee fans were locked out. A couple of hours later their anger had probably given way to relief — Motherwell won 4-0. Billy Steel's influence had been restricted by aggression and sound team work and the key players — Cox, Humphries and Watson — were to be found in the Motherwell ranks. Watson scored the crucial first goal in the Final and five in the competition as a whole. A sound Cup side, Motherwell had won the League Cup Final against Hibs by three goals to nil the previous season.

Falkirk had seemed doomed when, in February of 1957, they had only taken 13 points from 23 matches. An Englishman called Reggie Smith was persuaded to leave Dundee

United to manage Falkirk. The change was dramatic. A new spirit was instilled and two veterans, Andy Irvine and George Merchant, were signed and introduced to the side. The team fought their way to the Cup Final. At the end of the first game they were level with Kilmarnock at 1-1 and the score was the same at the end of normal time in the replay. Extra-time took place amid darkness as Hampden had no floodlights then. The hard-working Dougie Moran forced his way through the centre of a tiring defence and fired the ball past the Kilmarnock keeper, Jimmy Brown. A League victory a few days after the replay staved off relegation and completed the process of transformation.

Saint Mirren reached the Final in 1959 by beating Celtic 4-0 in the semi-final and found themselves playing Aberdeen. The most exciting feature of the side was the inside-forward trio of Tommy Bryceland, Gerry Baker and Tommy Gemmell. Two of them, Bryceland and Baker, scored in the Final, Saint Mirren winning 3-1.

For Celtic, then managed by Jimmy McGrory, the twenty years which followed the war were bleak ones punctuated by mysterious moments of brilliance. In the '50s the theo-

Above: *Falkirk. Scottish Cup-winners of 1957.*
Back row L. to R.: Godfrey (Trainer), Parker, Rae, Slater, Wright,
Irvine, Prentice, Smith (Manager).
Front row: Murray, Grierson, Merchant, Moran, O'Hara, McIntosh.

Below: *St. Mirren. Scottish Cup winners of 1959.*
Back row L. to R.: Wilson, Baker, Walker, Neilson, McGugan,
Leishman.
Front row: Rodger, Bryceland, Lapsley, Gemmell, Miller.

logically minded referred to their forwards as the "Five Sorrowful Mysteries". Yet there were some famous names in their team. There was the eccentric, nonchalantly skilled figure of Charlie Tully — who twice scored direct from the same corner when the referee ruled that it had to be retaken. In complete contrast there was, in midfield, the stalwart figure of Bobby Evans. While the club lacked the strength in depth to take trophies on any sort of regular basis, the intermittent successes tended to be on the grand scale. To celebrate the Coronation a football competition was played in Glasgow in 1953. Celtic hardly deserved their place in the illustrious company who played for the trophy but, as well as being crowd-pullers, they had, after all, won the previous all-British competitions in Scotland — the British League Cup and the Empire Exhibition Cup. They took the Coronation Cup. Celtic and Hibs, having beaten Manchester United and Newcastle United, respectively, contested the Final. A blistering shot by Mochan won Celtic the game but it was goalkeeper Bonnar, whose mistake helped Clyde in the 1955 Cup Final, who kept Hibs at bay. A late second produced the slightly deceptive scoreline of 2-0.

The centre-half in the team was Jock Stein. He had been brought from the obscurity of Llanelli to play for the club. More of a pragmatist than a stylist, he occasionally dismayed the cognoscenti by kneeing the ball clear, but he was to prove a sound defender. He captained Celtic to the double in season 1953-54.

Celtic's other major moment of elation came when, led by centre-forward Billy McPhail, they tore Rangers apart to win the League Cup of season 1957-58 by seven goals to one. They did not, however, win another major trophy until 1965.

McGrory's managerial career did have success. In the late '50s and early '60s he brought some good players to the club: Simpson, Craig, Gemmell, Murdoch, McNeill, Clark, Johnstone, Chalmers, Auld, Lennox, Hughes . . .

One of Celtic's moments of depression came when, during three hours of football, goalkeeper Eddie Connachan of Dunfermline denied them. His club won the replay of the 1961 Cup Final 2-0. The manager of Dunfermline was Jock Stein and his team preparation was so astute that some in football, a game too often crippled by its faith in tradition, thought it humorous. He prepared his side for a Cup-tie on a 'tight' ground, for example, by having them play in a reduced training area. Under George Farm's management Dunfermline were again to take the Cup, by beating Hearts in 1968. European football became a normal element of the fixture list for the Dunfermline of the 1960s.

Stein moved on to manage Hibs before returning to Celtic in March 1965 where he was guaranteed the kind of complete control of playing matters which McGrory had never had. Stein was partly a product of, and partly shaped, the revolution which saw directors concede power to the managers they appointed.

Top right: *Connachan of Dunfermline saves from Fernie of Celtic in the 1961 Scottish Cup Final.* Glasgow Herald.

Bottom right L. to R.: *Jock Stein congratulates his Dunfermline players Mailer and Miller on their Cup success against Celtic.* Glasgow Herald.

Below: *Jock Stein in action for Celtic.* Glasgow Herald.

Below: *Charlie Tully practising his famous corner kick.*

There has never been any lack of critics of Scottish football but it is to its enormous credit that the most cherished match in its history involved no Scottish player. In the European Cup Final of 1960 Real Madrid and Eintracht played what many consider to be the finest game ever seen. Eintracht had decimated Rangers with an aggregate victory of 12-4 in the semi-final, but their excellence proved no defence against Real. With Di Stefano orchestrating the moves and Puskas and Gento playing brilliantly in the attack Real won 7-3.

To be defeated by such a team was an honour and the stock of Eintracht was high enough for them to be brought back the following year to play Rangers in a match inaugurating the floodlights at Hampden.

Right: *Di Stefano (left) and Puskas at the end of the European Cup Final of 1960.* Glasgow Herald.

Below: *Di Stefano scores Real Madrid's seventh goal.* Glasgow Herald.

Above: *Celebrations following Puskas's fourth goal of the match (Real Madrid's sixth).* Glasgow Herald.

Above: *Billy McNeill of Celtic*. Glasgow Herald.

Left: *Jimmy Johnstone rounds Dave Mackay in the Queen's Park centenary match, 1967. Celtic v. Spurs*. Glasgow Herald.

Below: *Bertie Auld of Celtic*. Glasgow Herald.

Below right: *Bobby Murdoch of Celtic*. Glasgow Herald.

The Modern Game
1965 – 1984

The Stein era, properly speaking, began when a late goal by Billy McNeill gave Celtic a 3-2 victory in the Scottish Cup Final of 1965. Everyone knew there were players of promise at Celtic Park — they had reached the semi-finals of the Cup Winners' Cup in 1963-64 — but the win at Hampden suggested that achievement would replace potential. It did so with a vengeance. John Rafferty in his book *100 Years of Scottish Football,* called the Celtic side of that period "the greatest club team of the whole century" and that tribute seems no more than their due.

Stein's triumph lay in the way in which he made the kind of fine adjustments to the team which ensured maximum use of individual strengths and protected individual weaknesses. In midfield, Murdoch was pulled a little deeper and the extra time on the ball this gave him allowed the soundness of his passing technique to be employed to greater advantage. Celtic rarely gave the ball away in their own half. Complementing him was the more cunning figure of Bertie Auld. He had started his career as a winger with Celtic but his maverick temperament had led to his transfer to Birmingham. On his return to Parkhead he was still a winger but Stein saw the importance of utilising his skilful arrogance in a more central role and played him in midfield.

In defence, the already impressive centre-back partnership of Billy McNeill and John Clark was reinforced by the introduction of the veteran Ronnie Simpson in goals. Ironically, it had been Stein, as manager of Hibs, who had sold Simpson to Celtic. Simpson, whose father had been an excellent centre-half with Rangers, had a vast amount of experience. He had made his League debut with Queen's Park in 1946 at the tender age of 15. As far back as 1948 he had given Celtic cause to admire his skills. In a Glasgow Cup-tie they twice failed to beat him with penalties as he gave a headline-claiming display.

The forward line included the hard working and able figures of Bobby Lennox, Stevie Chalmers and Willie Wallace. The latter, a purchase from Hearts, proved a shrewd acquisition when the team was hit by the injury to the prolific Joe McBride at the end of 1966. Life was made easier for them by the fact that Stein at last produced some semblance of consistency in Jimmy Johnstone.

Johnstone's fiery spirit had, in his earlier days, too frequently manifested itself in physical confrontation. Under Stein he was coaxed and threatened into concentrating on using his marvellous abilities. Johnstone had the rare ability to send defenders the wrong way. Time and again his superb balance allowed him to leave defenders moving one way while he went the other. At his best, the joyous impudence with which he would 'show' the ball to an opponent before leaving him for dead was one of the finest sights the game has known.

The Final of the European Cup was reached and Celtic played Inter Milan in Lisbon in May 1967. Inter Milan, guided by the sterile ingenuity of manager Helenio Herrera, had discovered that man-to-man marking could be combined with the use of the "libero" (sweeper) to produce a watertight defence. This distasteful invention had taken them far but Europe longed to see them beaten.

After seven minutes Celtic were a goal down when right-back Jim Craig brought down Cappellini and Mazzola converted the penalty. Celtic had determined to attack but that goal turned choice into necessity.

Above: *Celtic train in Lisbon on the eve of the European Cup Final.* Glasgow Herald.

Below: *Gemmell scores in the European Cup Final, 1967.* Daily Express.

Right: *Chalmers scores the winner in the European Cup Final, 1967.* Daily Express.

The all-round strength of the Celtic side can be judged by the fact that it was the two full-backs, the cultured Craig and the flamboyant Tommy Gemmell, who carried the game to Inter Milan. The Italians seemed unable to cope with this. The width of Celtic's play in attack stretched their defence, preventing them from simply concentrating their forces in the centre. Chance after chance came to Celtic but it seemed for a long time that the athletic Sarti would save any shot that was on target.

Celtic at last broke through with a goal fashioned by the two full-backs. Craig moved inside a little and drew a few defenders before rolling the ball across to Gemmell. From 20 yards he lashed the ball into the keeper's top right-hand corner. With six minutes to go Chalmers re-directed a Murdoch shot and Celtic had won the greatest victory any Scottish club has ever known.

Celtic set what looks to be an unbeatable target by winning nine league titles in a row (1965-66 to 1973-74) and Stein, in that period, brought to the club players who seemed capable of equalling the success of Lisbon. It did not work out. Stars like Hay, Macari and Dalglish were lost to England while others did not fulfill their abundant promise. Saddest of all, the most naturally gifted player of that group, George Connelly, chose for personal reasons to abandon his career with the club.

It seemed that Celtic might take the European Cup again when they played Feyenoord in the Final of the 1970 competition. The team had aged by that time and what had

been gained in experience had been lost in enthusiasm. They were comprehensively outplayed although they lost by only two goals to one. Celtic's only consolation was their victory in the semi-finals against Leeds United. The English side had been regarded by the national press as certain winners of the tie. Celtic, however, followed their 1-0 win at Leeds with a 2-1 win at Hampden in front of an ecstatic crowd of more than 134,000.

On the domestic front there was much for Celtic fans to enjoy. The astute Stein signed "Dixie" Deans from Motherwell in 1971 for £17,500. Deans's disciplinary record had caused many to despair of him but Stein exercised a large measure of control over him and the chunky, competitive forward, whose ability in the air was ludicrously at odds with his small stature, was to score hat-tricks against Hibs in the Scottish Cup Final of 1972 and the League Cup Final of season 1974-75. The distinction of being the scorer of a hat-trick in a Scottish Cup Final is one which he shares with Jimmy Quinn alone. In the 1970s Celtic fans also witnessed the emergence of the most gifted British player of the period — Kenny Dalglish. The other important figure to come into the side in Stein's time was the current Celtic captain Danny McGrain, whose willingness to remain in, and star in, Scottish football has been sadly untypical.

Season 1977-78 saw Celtic without the services of Pat Stanton (who had, following his signing from Hibs, greatly strengthened the club's defence) and Danny McGrain. They had both sustained serious injuries and Stanton's career was

effectively ended. The transfer of Dalglish just before the beginning of that season meant that Celtic had lost their three best players. It was time for a new beginning at the club and Billy McNeill took over Stein's post in 1978. Under him Celtic won three league titles (1978-79, 1980-81, 1981-82) but success in Europe proved elusive. Rumours persisted that McNeill and the Celtic board existed in an uneasy relationship. They seemed to be proved correct when, during the summer of 1983, the club curtly rejected his request for a salary review and contract. McNeill left for Manchester City and was replaced by David Hay. Hay found himself dealing with a crisis. Charlie Nicholas had gone to Arsenal and George McCluskey followed him South a few days after Hay's appointment.

Hay's first season in charge was one in which the pleasures were incidental but the disappointments substantial. Brian McClair, McNeill's last signing for the club, scored 30 domestic goals in his first season of full-time football but Celtic could take only second prize in each of the major trophies. A considerable re-building job lay ahead.

Top left: *Celtic's return to Glasgow after the European Cup Final win, 1967. Glasgow Herald.*

Bottom left: *McNeill, Murdoch, Hughes and Williams celebrate Celtic's victory over Leeds at Hampden in 1970. Glasgow Herald.*

Right: *Danny McGrain of Celtic. Glasgow Herald.*

Below: *Dalglish of Celtic being challenged by Miller of Rangers. Glasgow Herald.*

Hat-trick by Dixie Deans in the 1972 Scottish Cup Final. Glasgow Herald.

Above: *Deans scores his first goal.*

Below: *Deans scores his second.*
Right: *Deans scores his third.*

Below: *John Hughes congratulates Kai Johansen and Ronnie McKinnon. 1966 Scottish Cup Final replay. Rangers have won 1-0 through a goal by Johansen.* Glasgow Herald.

For most of Stein's time with Celtic, Rangers were forced into the kind of role Celtic filled in the forties and fifties: their fans suffered a diet of failure punctuated by the occasional dramatic success. The week after Celtic had played in Lisbon, Rangers were in the Final of the Cup Winners' Cup. Cruel luck meant that they found themselves playing Bayern Munich in Nuremberg. The Rangers team was massively criticised as cumbersome and leaden-footed but they nonetheless might have won the Final. A goal in extra-time beat them.

They had qualified for that competition when their full-back Kai Johansen scored the only goal with a superb 20 yarder in their replayed Scottish Cup Final against Celtic. That was Scot Symon's last success as a manager. Rangers were beaten by Berwick Rangers in a Cup-tie on January 28th 1967 and Symon was sacked in September of that year. The assistant manager, Dave White, took over the post. In November 1969 White, in turn, was sacked. In December Willie Waddell, who had been employed in journalism since leaving Kilmarnock, took over and things slowly began to improve for Rangers. His appointment as coach was Jock Wallace, the man who had been Berwick's goalkeeper when they beat Rangers.

Waddell had taken the job at the most difficult time in the club's history and he was in charge when 66 people died in a disaster which occurred as Rangers fans who were leaving Ibrox tried to turn back when they heard the roar that signified that their side had scored an equaliser against

Above: *Colin Stein scores his first for Rangers in the 1972 Cup Winners' Cup Final*. Glasgow Herald.

Top right: *Willie Johnston with the Cup Winners' Cup*. Glasgow Herald.

Bottom right: *Celebrations at Ibrox the day after Rangers's Cup Winners' Cup victory*. Glasgow Herald.

Celtic. Those events of January 2nd 1971 made football seem something of an irrelevance.

Season 1971-72 saw Rangers at last take a European trophy. Waddell had a good team which was not inclined to wilt under pressure. Their defence included such reliable players as Peter McCloy, Sandy Jardine, Ronnie McKinnon and, after McKinnon suffered a broken leg, Colin Jackson. The whole was organised and controlled by the elegant Dave Smith. In midfield there was the hard working Alex McDonald and the perceptive Tommy McLean. Up front Rangers had the searing pace of Willie Johnston and the strength of Colin Stein (who had been the first £100,000 signing between Scottish clubs when he joined Rangers from Hibs in 1968).

Rangers went through the Cup Winners' Cup competition of 1971-72 with an impressive run of victories, the greatest of which was a 2-0 win at Ibrox over a Bayern Munich team which was shortly to win the European Cup three times in a row. The Final in Barcelona found Rangers playing their famous opponents of 1945 — Moscow Dynamo.

Everything went wrong for Rangers as they prepared for the game. Jackson failed to shake off an injury picked up in training and his place went to Derek Johnstone. John Greig, too, was injured and although he played it was clear that he was not fully fit. However, in the match itself Rangers's attitude was perfect as they swept to a 3-0 lead. After 24 minutes Stein took a Jardine pass and burst through the Dynamo defence to score a superb goal. Five minutes from

the interval Willie Johnston scored with, of all things, a neat header and five minutes after the break he scored a third. Moscow Dynamo came back into the game with two late goals, but Rangers, who had dominated so much of the match, thoroughly deserved their win. It was sad that crowd invasions during the match and pitched battle after it marred their victory, for their achievement had been great.

After Barcelona, Willie Waddell became the club's general manager while Jock Wallace took over the running of the team. The gruelling training routines Wallace devised for his side were mocked by many, but they did more than simply improve players' stamina, they increased the team's confidence by making them feel that they had the physical resources to overcome any challenge. Under Wallace, Rangers took the treble in seasons 1975-76 and 1977-78.

In that period two players who have since become Ibrox folk heroes emerged. Derek Johnstone made an immediate impact on Scottish football. As a sixteen year old his header gave Rangers a 1-0 victory against Celtic in the League Cup Final of season 1970-71, and he had gone on to win his Cup Winners' Cup Medal as a centre-half in 1972. Under Wallace he emerged, however, as an out-and-out forward. The service of Tommy McLean helped Johnstone, a superb header of the ball, to become a prolific scorer. Defences were to discover that he could also display, when required, an extremely deft touch on the ground.

Wallace's other 'find' was Tom Forsyth, whom he signed from Motherwell in October 1972. Forsyth was never any-

Above: *Derek Johnstone heads the only goal of the 1970-71 League Cup Final.* Glasgow Herald.

Top right: *Tom Forsyth scores the winner in the 1973 Scottish Cup Final against Celtic.* Glasgow Herald.

Bottom right: *Jock Wallace congratulates Alex MacDonald at the end of the 1973 Scottish Cup Final.* Glasgow Herald.

one's idea of a ball-player but he entered the ranks of legend with the club by nervously bumping the ball over the line from a couple of yards to score the winner in Rangers's 3-2 Scottish Cup win over Celtic in 1973. Although feared for the extreme hardness of his play he was, nonetheless, an accomplished tackler. His brilliant tackle on Mike Channon, which preserved Scotland's 2-1 lead in the England game of 1976, is as warmly remembered as any goal against the "Old Enemy".

Wallace took up the post of manager of Leicester in 1978 and John Greig retired as a player and replaced him at Ibrox. He found himself in command of a team which had been allowed to grow old together and he was, accordingly, forced into the transfer market. Greig brought Rangers Cup success, but consistency in the League eluded him. Greig's signings consistently failed to perform to standards they had previously established. John McClelland was the splendid exception. Signed for a modest £80,000 from Mansfield he went on to marshall Northern Ireland's defence during their proud performance in the 1982 World Cup.

It was McClelland who was Jock Wallace's major asset when he returned to the club to replace Greig early in season 1983-84. Rangers regrouped sufficiently to win the League Cup with a 3-2 victory over Celtic. A Greig signing, McCoist, scored a hat-trick. For Wallace the victory was

only a down payment on larger successes he intended to bring. Despite doubts over McClelland's future with the club, Rangers seemed set to grow stronger. The signing of forward Iain Ferguson from Dundee in the summer of 1984 was a statement of intent.

Between seasons 1970-71 and 1978-79 every league title and Scottish Cup was won by either Celtic or Rangers. The best hope for the others lay in the League Cup — especially if Celtic were the opposition. From season 1971-72 to 1973-74 Celtic lost the League Cup Final to, respectively, Partick Thistle, Hibernian and Dundee.

The first of these defeats saw Thistle chalk up an unbelievable 4-1 victory. Crowds around Scotland had greeted news of Thistle's 4-0 half-time lead with derision and disbelief. Thistle's newly promoted team, though, contained the kind of mixture which was naturally given to the occasional explosion.

The young Alan Rough was an exciting goalkeeper and in front of him there was a future Scotland international, John Hansen. In the centre of defence the veteran Hugh Strachan brought vital experience to the side. There were plenty of possible goalscorers in the team with Jimmy Bone and Frank Coulston forming a substantial threat in attack. On the wing they had Denis McQuade. He was the kind of winger who could, at times, appear to be playing with complete indiffer-

Above: *Lawrie scores Thistle's second goal in the 1971-72 League Cup Final.* Glasgow Herald.

Below: *The return to Firhill after Partick Thistle's League Cup victory. At first the key to the main door could not be found.* Glasgow Herald.

ence to the position of the goals and the necessity of scoring. On other occasions he was lethal.

Thistle's assault staggered Celtic to the extent that Jimmy Bone was able to run through a frozen Celtic defence to score the fourth with laughable simplicity. The Thistle mixture, however, could go wrong. Sometimes the experienced seemed simply old and the erratic were simply awful. The week after Thistle beat Celtic they lost 7-2 to Aberdeen. Perhaps the celebrations had gone on a little too long.

Hibs's League Cup victory the following season was to be the only reward for a team which was dazzling in the early '70s. With players such as Brownlie, Blackley, Stanton, Cropley, O'Rourke and Gordon they had quality in every section of the team. They also had an unfortunate tendency to be thrashed by Celtic. Deans, as mentioned, was in the habit of scoring hat-tricks against them. They briefly broke the spell, however, when goals by Stanton and O'Rourke won them the League Cup Final of season 1972-73.

Dundee became the next team to break through when they outlasted Celtic in atrocious conditions of rain and cold to score a late goal when the durable and alert Gordon Wallace turned cleverly to score with a low shot. Dundee's captain that day was the former Celtic full-back Tommy Gemmell. Celtic fans had been pleased to see him return to the Scottish scene from England but became less pleased when they realised that he had lost little of his competitive spirit.

Above: *Gordon Wallace (No. 9) scores the only goal of the 1973-74 League Cup Final. The driving rain has soaked Hunter's goalkeeper's jersey revealing the hooped top he was wearing beneath.*

Below: *Dundee skipper Tommy Gemmell with the League Cup. Glasgow Herald.*

The League Cup was also, in season 1969-70, the occasion for St. Johnstone to give evidence of the abilities of their manager, Willie Ormond. They reached the Final of the competition before losing 1-0 to Celtic. Ormond's side was an effective one and they were to have a brief but exciting European run which included the defeat of mighty Hamburg. It had been an astute use of limited resources which brought St. Johnstone the third place in the League which took them into Europe and Ormond's talents did not pass unnoticed.

The national team had occasional moments of joy in its otherwise distracted and meandering progress through the 1960s. In 1966 Italy were beaten in a World Cup qualifying match at Hampden, when John Greig burst through to score the game's only goal. The following year England were the opponents at Wembley. Scotland fielded a makeshift side playing its first game under a new manager (Bobby Brown) against the World Champions. The adverse circumstances seemed only to inspire Scotland. England were humiliated but Scotland did not press the point and won by only three goals to two. England's decline at international level in the '70s changed the focus of our efforts. At last, we came to measure ourselves by the standards of the World Cup.

Willie Ormond took over the management of the side from Tommy Docherty in 1973. His first game was against England, in a match celebrating the S.F.A.'s centenary. Scotland lost 5-0. This proved to be a blessing in disguise for Ormond, although he might have said that he would have preferred his blessings straight. It gave him the mandate to completely rebuild the side. The canniness he had gained as manager of St. Johnstone stood him in good stead.

Top left: *Denis Law in action against England at Hampden in 1962. John White (left) and Pat Crerand look on. White was tragically killed by lightning in 1964.* Glasgow Herald.

Bottom left: *Denis Law soars above Bobby Moore to score against England at Hampden in 1966.* Glasgow Herald.

Above: *Joe Jordan scores the goal against Czechoslovakia which took Scotland to the 1974 World Cup Finals.* Glasgow Herald.

Below: *Bremner of Leeds explains to Mackay of Spurs that it is all a misunderstanding. Two of the competitive Scots who have enriched English football.* Syndication International.

The side he built possessed the pleasing, if un-Scottish, virtue of solidity. In goals there was David Harvey, a keeper given to making few mistakes. The full-back partnership of Sandy Jardine and Danny McGrain let little past, although McGrain's selection on the left meant that he was less able to display his attacking skills. In the centre of the defence was the awesome figure, beloved of the fans, of Jim Holton. He appeared, at times, to be crude but was to prove more than adequate at the highest level. In midfield there was Bremner. His career with Leeds had given him experience both of struggling at a crude, hard level of the game and, later, playing against the best in Europe. Under Ormond the competitive and creative sides of his game were both given expression. Beside him was David Hay. Hay's willingness to push himself to the physical limit meant that he not only reinforced the attack but also managed to cover in defence. His qualities, it is widely thought, have been sorely missed by Scotland teams since. Up front the figure of Joe Jordan came to the fore. Jordan's ferocious devotion to the cause reversed the normal intimidatory relationship that exists between defenders and forwards.

The moment of breakthrough came when Holton and Jordan, who had come on as substitute, scored against Czechoslovakia in 1973 and ensured Scotland's participation in the World Cup in West Germany the following year.

Scotland went through the tournament undefeated, beating Zaire 2-0 and drawing with Brazil (0-0) and Yugoslavia (1-1). In these three games, Hay and Bremner had struck

many as being amongst the best players in the World Cup. Despite being the only undefeated team in the tournament (the winners, West Germany, lost a match against East Germany) Scotland were knocked out on goal difference. Scotland's goal in the Yugoslavia game had been created by the often inspired figure of Hutchison who had come on as substitute. A feeling persists that Hutchison or Jimmy Johnstone, had they been played in the games, might have brought a crucial element of inspiration to Scotland's play.

It must be said, though, that Ormond's record in major matches is unequalled by any other Scottish manager of modern times. Ormond, regrettably, tended to be plagued by trivial but newsworthy controversies involving his players. In 1974 Johnstone, after some late night high-jinks, had to be rescued from a rowing boat that went adrift. This would barely seem worthy of comment if the incident involved a Rugby team. The press, however, had a field day. It should be noted that Johnstone was, three days later, a key figure in a 2-0 victory over England. Perhaps boating escapades should be compulsory for Scotland players. Ormond, an unassertive person, did not trouble to defend himself when attacked by the press. Eventually support for him in the S.F.A. itself grew weak. There seemed to be a feeling that Scotland should have a more flamboyant and publicity conscious manager.

Ormond resigned in 1977 and Ally MacLeod took over. He inherited a splendid team, based on the skills of Bruce Rioch and Don Masson in midfield, which reached its peak

Above: *Bremner narrowly fails to score against Brazil in the 1974 World Cup. Scotland drew 0-0.* Glasgow Herald.

Bottom left: *Dalglish considers Holton's footwork.* Glasgow Herald.

Below: *Jordan scores against Yugoslavia in the 1974 World Cup.* Glasgow Herald.

with a sophisticated victory over England in 1977. Sadly the form of Masson and Rioch went into rapid decline in the year which followed. MacLeod, though, had convinced a nation, who wished to be convinced of such a thing, that Scotland were a great team and, having said so, he was not prepared to recognise the necessity of rebuilding the side. The team was further damaged when McGrain, then at the height of his powers, sustained a serious injury which kept him out of the World Cup.

In Argentina Scotland's level of performance was simply mediocre — they took three points from three games — but in comparison to the nation's expectations it was a disaster. Worse than the results was the fact that Willie Johnston had been found to have stupidly taken an innocuous but illegal stimulant. There was the glorious consolation of seeing Archie Gemmill score the tournament's best goal as Scotland beat Holland 3-2. The dream-like ease with which he ended his solo run by chipping the ball into the goals is a permanent addition to the memory of everyone who saw it.

Ally MacLeod had proved himself as a manager with Ayr United and Aberdeen and his miscalculations at international level were punished with an undeserved severity.

Jock Stein took over a side for which the nation, too hurt by Argentina, no longer wished to risk enthusiasm. Stein attempted to rebuild by creating a solid and wary side, and he achieved this aim to the extent that they carefully and competently picked their way through the qualifying matches and secured their passage to Spain.

Then, things went wrong. In an attempt to boost the team's performance Stein introduced Evans of Aston Villa. He was dropped after the first World Cup match against New Zealand. The new central defensive partnership was Miller and Hansen. They, as had been clear from their first game together against Belgium in 1979, were too similar to play well together. To make matters worse the team lacked a midfield player prepared to cover in defence. In particular, the vital second goals scored by Brazil and Russia in our matches against them would have produced acrimony and accusation in a team of schoolboys.

On the positive side, Scotland scored eight goals in three games and the cleverness which produced them showed that Stein had performed successful work as he prepared the team for Spain. The heartbreak of failing to beat Russia in the vital third game was tempered by the satisfying thought that Scotland had at least sought to entertain.

After Spain, Scotland's glazed trudge out of their European Championship qualifying section left the fans clinging to the hope that the prospect of the '86 World Cup would stiffen the resolve and quicken the pace.

Surely, it is time to allow a smidgin of wild optimism back into our game. Prolonged exposure to sanity can be debilitating.

One particularly satisfying trend in Scotland's international selections has been the increasing presence of 'home' Scots. The Premier League, introduced in season 1975-76, deserves much of the credit for this. It has produced the kind of regular intense competition which has forced the teams outside the Old Firm either to compete vigorously or see themselves relegated. At the time of writing, Aberdeen and Dundee United are the best teams in Scotland. In the early '70s such a situation was unimaginable.

In the mid '60s Dundee United gained a certain amount of glamour and success by introducing four Scandinavian players to their side. A number of such players were brought

**Scotland's goals in their 3-2 victory over Holland.
World Cup 1978.** Glasgow Herald.

Left: *Dalglish scores the first.*
Top: *Gemmill scores the second.*
Right: *Gemmill scores the third.*

Above: *Scotland celebrates Narey's goal against Brazil in the World Cup Finals.* Glasgow Herald.

Below: *Chivadze scores Russia's first goal against Scotland in the 1982 World Cup Finals. Hansen, Robertson, and Rough lament.* Glasgow Herald.

Above: *Nicholas scores his first goal for Scotland, against Switzerland, March 30th 1983. Glasgow Herald.*

Below: *Finn Dossing, who scored twenty-one goals for Dundee United in his first twenty matches for the club. Glasgow Herald.*

to Scottish football at the time but Dundee United and Morton pursued the policy more enthusiastically than any of the others. United remedied their poor position at the half-way stage in season 1964-65 by signing Persson, Dossing, Berg and Wing. Dossing scored 21 goals in his first 20 appearances and the club took 28 points from their last 17 League fixtures. United further caught the eye by being one of the Scottish sides which, in the close seasons of the late '60s, played for American towns in football tournaments. The meeting in 1969 of Dundee United of Dallas and Kilmarnock of St. Louis, to take one example from what was an odd competition, must be the strangest encounter those sides have known.

Under Jim McLean Dundee United won a reputation for playing the purest football in Scotland. In seasons 1979-80 and 1980-81 they won the League Cup (their victories being against Aberdeen and Dundee) but many doubted their ability to take the Scottish Cup or the League. It was commonly felt that they lacked staying power. In season 1982-83 the club at last silenced their critics.

In the U.E.F.A. Cup of season 1981-82 they had astonished the football world by thrashing Borussia Moenchengladbach by 5-0. They carried that kind of form into the vital games of the next League campaign. Their team had been strengthened by the emergence of Gough and Milne to lend support to such fine players as Narey, Bannon and Sturrock. Still, it seemed at times that United would not succeed, but marvellous victories at Celtic Park and Pittodrie kept them in the hunt and their win at Dens Park on the final day of the season brought them the League. Curiously, United have had their three major trophy wins on the ground of their neighbours.

115

Dundee United beat Borussia Moenchengladbach 5-0 in the U.E.F.A. Cup of season 1981-82. Frank Tocher.

Above: *Milne scores the first.*
Below: *Kirkwood scores the second.*
Top right: *Sturrock scores the third.*
Bottom right: *Hegarty scores the fourth.*
Top (page 118): *Bannon scores the fifth.*

Ralph Milne had laid claim to the title of United's key player by scoring in each of those three crucial League games and it was he who set confidence flowing through United in their subsequent European run. He scored twice in a 4-0 victory at Tannadice as United's momentum and pace all but incinerated Standard Liege. The European matches, however, were to reveal the quality and effectiveness of the entire side. In the first leg of the semi-final it was goals by Dodds and Stark, too easily thought of as bit-players, which brought a 2-0 victory over Roma. The lead proved an inadequate bulwark against their own inexperience and the precise skills of a team which knew the Final was to be played in their own city. The plutocrats won 3-0. Nonetheless, United could relish the fact that it had been ten years since a Scottish side had last reached the semi-finals of the European Cup.

For Aberdeen, a new era had seemed to arrive when they beat Celtic in the 1970 Scottish Cup Final. They had such stars as the accomplished Martin Buchan, who was captaining them at the age of 21, and that lethal finisher, Joe Harper. The man who did most to bring Aberdeen the Cup, however, was Derek McKay who scored twice in the Final. He was to do little for the club thereafter but doubtless the Aberdeen supporters judge his career to have been satisfactory. Surprisingly, Aberdeen did not manage to maintain any great level of success in the 1970s and they won only the League Cup (in season 1976-77). The fact that they lost Buchan to Manchester United in 1972 seemed to sap the club's strength.

In 1978 Alex Ferguson, a former Rangers player, became manager of the club in succession to Billy McNeill. In a remarkably brief time he gave Aberdeen the greatest side in the club's history. In season 1979-80 they powered their way past a faltering Celtic to take the League title. This time they built on success. The international centre-back partnership of McLeish and Miller gave the team a solid defence. In midfield, the introduction of Simpson and Cooper meant that few teams would ever be likely to wrest control of that area. With their physical reinforcement it became easier for Gordon Strachan to display all his energetic skills. Further forward the signing of McGhee and Weir and the emergence of Black and Hewitt gave Aberdeen an unmatched richness of striking talent.

Having won the Scottish Cup in 1982 they followed it with the Cup Winners' Cup in 1983. In the minds of many the loss of Scottish talents to England — most recently seen in the cases of Charlie Nicholas and Maurice Johnston — had led to the conviction that Scotland could no longer hope for European success. Aberdeen emphatically changed all that. In their quarter-final tie they had been losing 2-1 to Bayern Munich with twelve minutes to go. Late goals by McLeish and substitute Hewitt brought the win that was needed. This was a team which seemed immune to the normal Scottish tendency to fail.

For the Final in Gothenburg, against Real Madrid, Aberdeen were without Stewart Kennedy and the man who had almost single-handedly disposed of Waterschei in the semi-finals, Dougie Bell. Such was the depth of the Aberdeen pool

Above: *Milne scores in Dundee United's vital League win over Aberdeen at Pittodrie, March 1983.* Sports Projects.

Below: *Harper scores from the spot against Celtic in Aberdeen's 1970 Scottish Cup Final victory.* Glasgow Herald.

that these losses, sad though they were, did not weaken the team.

In the Final itself Aberdeen comprehensively beat Real Madrid and gave Scottish football its greatest night in a decade. From shortly after Black's opening goal Real Madrid seemed to accept that they could not hope to win. They cravenly defended, after they had been gifted an undeserved equaliser, in the hope that they might take the Final to that deplorable round of penalty kicks which brings an inane conclusion to so many vital games. They were foiled when Weir's beautifully judged chip sent McGhee clear, and his cross was headed in by the cool figure of John Hewitt, who had once again come off the bench to play a decisive role in a major game. The Cup Winners' Cup had been won by two goals to one.

Having put Scottish club football back on the international map Aberdeen went on to break new ground in their own patch. In 1984 they became only the second team this century to win three successive Scottish Cups. Their League win made them the first side outside the Old Firm to take the double. The departure of Strachan and McGhee which followed was a disappointment but their rivals had the lurking suspicion that the club had grown too strong to be broken by such derelictions. and their achievements demonstrated that our game was alive and well beyond the confines of Glasgow.

There is a tendency to pine for the huge crowds of the late '40s and '50s but no-one would wish to return to a period when the country was haunted by war and driven to football as a diversion from the austerity of an utterly crippled economy.

The rise in Premier League attendances of 155,716 in 1982-83, and of 160,093 in the following season, suggests that the game is in good health. In any case, football remains the currency of conversation in Scotland; a crucial element in the way we think and feel about ourselves.

Above: *Tensions on the Aberdeen bench in the 1983 Cup Winners' Cup Final.* Aberdeen Evening Express.

Bottom left: *Hewitt scores the winner against Bayern Munich in Aberdeen's Cup Winners' Cup quarter-final tie, 1983.* Sports Projects.

Below: *John Hewitt scores the winner over Real Madrid in the 1983 Cup Winners' Cup Final.* Aberdeen Evening Express.

Above: *Hewitt jumps for joy after scoring Aberdeen's winning goal against Real Madrid.* Aberdeen Evening Express.

Above: *McMaster and McLeish after the League win at Easter Road which brought Aberdeen the title in 1980. Frank Tocher.*

Below: *Eric Black scores the first goal in Aberdeen's 1984 Scottish Cup Final victory over Celtic. The ball has bounced behind keeper Bonner's body.*

Above: *The Scottish Cup.*
Above left: *The Scottish League Championship Trophy*

Scottish League and Cup Winners 1873–1984

Season	Scottish Cup	Scottish League	League Cup
1873–74	Queen's Park		
1874–75	Queen's Park		
1875–76	Queen's Park		
1876–77	Vale of Leven		
1877–78	Vale of Leven		
1878–79	Vale of Leven		
1879–80	Queen's Park		
1880–81	Queen's Park		
1881–82	Queen's Park		
1882–83	Dumbarton		
1883–84	Queen's Park		
1884–85	Renton		
1885–86	Queen's Park		
1886–87	Hibernian		
1887–88	Renton		
1888–89	Third Lanark		
1889–90	Queen's Park	**Scottish League**	
1890–91	Hearts	Dumbarton/Rangers	
1891–92	Celtic	Dumbarton	
1892–93	Queen's Park	Celtic	
		First Division	
1893–94	Rangers	Celtic	
1894–95	St. Bernards	Hearts	
1895–96	Hearts	Celtic	
1896–97	Rangers	Hearts	
1897–98	Rangers	Celtic	
1898–99	Celtic	Rangers	
1899–00	Celtic	Rangers	
1900–01	Hearts	Rangers	
1901–02	Hibernian	Rangers	
1902–03	Rangers	Hibernian	
1903–04	Celtic	Third Lanark	
1904–05	Third Lanark	Celtic	
1905–06	Hearts	Celtic	
1906–07	Celtic	Celtic	
1907–08	Celtic	Celtic	
1908–09	(1)	Celtic	
1909–10	Dundee	Celtic	
1910–11	Celtic	Rangers	
1911–12	Celtic	Rangers	
1912–13	Falkirk	Rangers	
1913–14	Celtic	Celtic	
1914–15	–	Celtic	
1915–16	–	Celtic	
1916–17	–	Celtic	
1917–18	–	Rangers	
1918–19	–	Celtic	
1919–20	Kilmarnock	Rangers	
1920–21	Partick Thistle	Rangers	
1921–22	Morton	Celtic	
1922–23	Celtic	Rangers	
1923–24	Airdrie	Rangers	
1924–25	Celtic	Rangers	
1925–26	St. Mirren	Celtic	
1926–27	Celtic	Rangers	
1927–28	Rangers	Rangers	
1928–29	Kilmarnock	Rangers	
1929–30	Rangers	Rangers	
1930–31	Celtic	Rangers	
1931–32	Rangers	Motherwell	
1932–33	Celtic	Rangers	
1933–34	Rangers	Rangers	
1934–35	Rangers	Rangers	
1935–36	Rangers	Celtic	
1936–37	Celtic	Rangers	
1937–38	East Fife	Celtic	
1938–39	Clyde	Rangers	**League Cup**
1946–47	Aberdeen	Rangers	Rangers
1947–48	Rangers	Hibernian	East Fife
1948–49	Rangers	Rangers	Rangers
1949–50	Rangers	Rangers	East Fife
1950–51	Celtic	Hibernian	Motherwell
1951–52	Motherwell	Hibernian	Dundee
1952–53	Rangers	Rangers	Dundee
1953–54	Celtic	Celtic	East Fife
1954–55	Clyde	Aberdeen	Hearts

(1) *The Cup was withheld after a riot followed the second drawn match between Celtic and Rangers.*

Season	Scottish Cup	Scottish League	League Cup
1955–56	Hearts	Rangers	Aberdeen
1956–57	Falkirk	Rangers	Celtic
1957–58	Clyde	Hearts	Celtic
1958–59	St. Mirren	Rangers	Hearts
1959–60	Rangers	Hearts	Hearts
1960–61	Dunfermline	Rangers	Rangers
1961–62	Rangers	Dundee	Rangers
1962–63	Rangers	Rangers	Hearts
1963–64	Rangers	Rangers	Rangers
1964–65	Celtic	Kilmarnock	Rangers
1965–66	Rangers	Celtic	Celtic
1966–67	Celtic	Celtic	Celtic
1967–68	Dunfermline	Celtic	Celtic
1968–69	Celtic	Celtic	Celtic
1969–70	Aberdeen	Celtic	Celtic
1970–71	Celtic	Celtic	Rangers
1971–72	Celtic	Celtic	Part. Thistle
1972–73	Rangers	Celtic	Hibernian
1973–74	Celtic	Celtic	Dundee
1974–75	Celtic	Rangers	Celtic
		Premier League	
1975–76	Rangers	Rangers	Rangers
1976–77	Celtic	Celtic	Aberdeen
1977–78	Rangers	Rangers	Rangers
1978–79	Rangers	Celtic	Rangers
1979–80	Celtic	Aberdeen	Dundee Un.
1980–81	Rangers	Celtic	Dundee Un.
1981–82	Aberdeen	Celtic	Rangers
1982–83	Aberdeen	Dundee Un.	Celtic
1983–84	Aberdeen	Aberdeen	Rangers

Bottom left: *Reunion of Vale of Leven players from the Cup-winning sides in Alloway in 1925. L. to R.: A. McLintock, James Ferguson, J. McPherson, J. McGregor, D. Lindsay, A. McIntyre, John Ferguson, James Ferguson is holding the "Loving Cup".*

Below: *Scottish League Cup*

Above: *Sammy Reid scores for Berwick and knocks Rangers out of the 1967 Scottish Cup*. Denis Straughan.

Below: *Reunion in 1947 of Morton players in 1922. The group includes H. Howatt (Trainer), J. Henry, (asst. Trainer), R. McGregor, James Gourlay, J. McIntyre, R. Brown, R. McKay, J. McMinn, W. Gibson, P. Thorpe, W. Allan, M. Watt. (Gibson, Thorpe, Allan and Watt did not play in the Final itself)*. Glasgow Herald.

Scotland's International Record November 1872 – June 1984

Date	Venue	Country	Result
30.11.72	Hamilton Cr.	England	D 0-0
8.3.73	The Oval	England	L 2-4
7.3.74	Hamilton Cr.	England	W 2-1
6.3.75	The Oval	England	D 2-2
4.3.76	Hamilton Cr.	England	W 3-0
25.3.76	Hamilton Cr.	Wales	W 4.0
3.3.77	The Oval	England	W 3-1
5.3.77	Wrexham	Wales	W 2-0
2.3.78	1st Ham'den	England	W 7-2
23.3.78	1st Ham'den	Wales	W 9-0
5.4.79	The Oval	England	L 4-5
7.4.79	Wrexham	Wales	W 3-0
13.3.80	1st Ham'den	England	W 5-4
27.3.80	1st Ham'den	Wales	W 5-1
12.3.81	The Oval	England	W 6-1
14.3.81	Wrexham	Wales	W 5-1
11.3.82	1st Ham'den	England	W 5-1
25.3.82	1st Ham'den	Wales	W 5-0
10.3.83	Bramall Lane	England	W 3-2
12.3.83	Wrexham	Wales	W 3-0
26.1.84	Belfast	Ireland	W 5-0
15.3.84	1st Cathkin	England	W 1-0
29.3.84	1st Cathkin	Wales	W 4-1
14.3.85	2nd Ham'den	Ireland	W 8-2
21.3.85	The Oval	England	D 1-1
23.3.85	Wrexham	Wales	W 8-1
20.3.86	Belfast	Ireland	W 7-2
27.3.86	2nd Ham'den	England	D 1-1
10.4.86	2nd Ham'den	Wales	W 4-1
19.2.87	2nd Ham'den	Ireland	W 4-1
19.3.87	Blackburn	England	W 3-2
21.3.87	Wrexham	Wales	W 2-0
10.3.88	Easter Road	Wales	W 5-1
17.3.88	2nd Ham'den	England	L 0-5
24.3.88	Cliftonville	Ireland	W 10-2
9.3.89	Ibrox	Ireland	W 7-0
13.4.89	The Oval	England	W 3-2
15.4.89	Wrexham	Wales	D 0-0
22.3.90	Paisley	Wales	W 5-0
29.3.90	Belfast	Ireland	W 4-1
5.4.90	2nd Ham'den	England	D 1-1
21.3.91	Wrexham	Wales	W 4-3
28.3.91	Parkhead	Ireland	W 2-1
4.4.91	Blackburn	England	L 1-2
19.3.92	Cliftonville	Ireland	W 3-2
26.3.92	Tynecastle	Wales	W 6-1
2.4.92	Ibrox	England	L 1-4
18.3.93	Wrexham	Wales	W 8-0
25.3.93	Parkhead	Ireland	W 6-1
1.4.93	Richmond	England	L 2-5
24.3.94	Kilmarnock	Wales	W 5-2
31.3.94	Cliftonville	Ireland	W 2-1
7.4.94	Parkhead	England	D 2-2
23.3.95	Wrexham	Wales	D 2-2
30.3.95	Parkhead	Ireland	W 3-1
6.4.95	Goodison	England	L 0-3
21.3.96	Carolina, D'dee	Wales	W 4-0
28.3.96	Cliftonville	Ireland	D 3-3
4.4.96	Parkhead	England	W 2-1
20.3.97	Wrexham	Wales	D 2-2
27.3.97	Ibrox	Ireland	W 5-1
3.4.97	Crystal Pal.	England	W 2-1
19.3.98	Motherwell	Wales	W 5-2
26.3.98	Cliftonville	Ireland	W 3-0
2.4.98	Parkhead	England	L 1-3
18.3.99	Wrexham	Wales	W 6-0
25.3.99	Parkhead	Ireland	W 9-1
8.4.99	Villa Park	England	L 1-2
3.2.00	Aberdeen	Wales	W 5-2
3.3.00	Cliftonville	Ireland	W 3-0
7.4.00	Parkhead	England	W 4-1
23.2.01	Parkhead	Ireland	W 11-0
2.3.01	Wrexham	Wales	D 1-1
30.3.01	Crystal Pal.	England	D 2-2
1.3.02	Belfast	Ireland	W 5-1
15.3.02	Greenock	Wales	W 5-1
3.5.02	Villa Park	England	D 2-2
9.3.03	Cardiff	Wales	W 1-0
21.3.03	Parkhead	Ireland	L 0-2
4.4.03	Bramall Lane	England	W 2-1
12.3.04	Dens Park	Wales	D 1-1
26.3.04	Dublin	Ireland	D 1-1
9.4.04	Parkhead	England	L 0-1
6.3.05	Wrexham	Wales	L 1-3
18.3.05	Parkhead	Ireland	W 4-0
1.4.05	Crystal Pal.	England	L 0-1
3.3.06	Tynecastle	Wales	L 0-2
17.3.06	Dublin	Ireland	W 1-0
7.4.06	Hampden	England	W 2-1
4.3.07	Wrexham	Wales	L 0-1
16.3.07	Parkhead	Ireland	W 3-0
6.4.07	Newcastle	England	D 1-1
7.3.08	Dens Park	Wales	W 2-1
14.3.08	Dublin	Ireland	W 5-0
4.4.08	Hampden	England	D 1-1
1.3.09	Wrexham	Wales	L 2-3
15.3.09	Ibrox	Ireland	W 5-0
3.4.09	Crystal Pal.	England	L 0-2
5.3.10	Kilmarnock	Wales	W 1-0

Below: A reunion in 1925 which included 10 of the Scotland side (v. England) of 1900. Back row L. to R.: R.S. McColl, Jacky Robertson, Alec Raisbeck, Bobby Walker, Walter Arnott. Front row: Harry Rennie, Johnny Campbell, Jack Bell, Neilly Gibson, R.C. Hamilton, Alec Smith, J. Drummond. The missing team member is Nicol Smith, who died of enteric fever in 1905. R.C. Hamilton did not play in the "Rosebery game" although he was capped that season. Walter Arnott (Queen's Park) played his last international in 1893. He was a great full-back, famous for the tremendous length of his clearances.

Date	Venue		Country	Result
19.3.10	Belfast		Ireland	L 0-1
2.4.10	Hampden		England	W 2-0
6.3.11	Cardiff		Wales	D 2-2
18.3.11	Parkhead		Ireland	W 2-0
1.4.11	Goodison		England	D 1-1
2.3.12	Tynecastle		Wales	W 1-0
16.3.12	Belfast		Ireland	W 4-1
23.3.12	Hampden		England	D 1-1
3.3.13	Wrexham		Wales	D 0-0
15.3.13	Dublin		Ireland	W 2-1
5.4.13	Stamford B.		England	L 0-1
28.2.14	Parkhead		Wales	D 0-0
14.3.14	Belfast		Ireland	D 1-1
4.4.14	Hampden		England	W 3-1
26.2.20	Cardiff		Wales	D 1-1
13.3.20	Parkhead		Ireland	W 3-0
10.4.20	Bramall Lane		England	L 4-5
12.2.21	Aberdeen		Wales	W 2-1
26.2.21	Belfast		N. Ireland	W 2-0
9.4.21	Hampden		England	W 3-0
4.2.22	Wrexham		Wales	L 1-2
4.3.22	Parkhead		N. Ireland	W 2-1
8.4.22	Villa Park		England	W 1-0
3.3.23	Belfast		N. Ireland	W 1-0
17.3.23	Paisley		Wales	W 2-0
14.4.23	Hampden		England	D 2-2
16.2.24	Cardiff		Wales	L 0-2
1.3.24	Parkhead		N. Ireland	W 2-0
12.4.24	Wembley		England	D 1-1
14.2.25	Tynecastle		Wales	W 3-1
28.2.25	Belfast		N. Ireland	W 3-0
4.4.25	Hampden		England	W 2-0
31.10.25	Cardiff		Wales	W 3-0
27.2.26	Ibrox		N. Ireland	W 4-0
17.4.26	Old Trafford		England	W 1-0
30.10.26	Ibrox		Wales	W 3-0
26.2.27	Belfast		N. Ireland	W 2-0
2.4.27	Hampden		England	L 1-2
29.10.27	Wrexham		Wales	D 2-2
25.2.28	Firhill		N. Ireland	L 0-1
31.3.28	Wembley		England	W 5-1
27.10.28	Ibrox		Wales	W 4-2
23.2.29	Belfast		N. Ireland	W 7-3
13.4.29	Hampden		England	W 1-0
26.5.29	Bergen		Norway	W 7-3
1.6.29	Berlin		Germany	D 1-1
4.6.29	Amsterdam		Holland	W 2-0
26.10.29	Cardiff		Wales	W 4-2
22.2.30	Parkhead		N. Ireland	W 3-1
5.4.30	Wembley		England	L 2-5
18.5.30	Paris		France	W 2-0
25.10.30	Ibrox		Wales	D 1-1
21.2.31	Belfast		N. Ireland	D 0-0
28.3.31	Hampden		England	W 2-0
16.5.31	Vienna		Austria	L 0-5
20.5.31	Rome		Italy	L 0-3
24.5.31	Geneva		Switzerland	W 3-2
19.9.31	Ibrox		N. Ireland	W 3-1
31.10.31	Wrexham		Wales	W 3-2
9.4.32	Wembley		England	L 0-3
8.5.32	Paris		France	W 3-1
17.9.32	Belfast		N. Ireland	W 4-0
26.10.32	Tynecastle		Wales	L 2-5
1.4.33	Hampden		England	W 2-1
16.9.33	Parkhead		N. Ireland	L 1-2
4.10.33	Cardiff		Wales	L 2-3
29.11.33	Hampden		Austria	D 2-2
14.4.34	Wembley		England	L 0-3
20.10.34	Belfast		N. Ireland	L 1-2
21.11.34	Pittodrie		Wales	W 3-2
6.4.35	Hampden		England	W 2-0
21.8.35	Hampden		England	W 4-2
5.10.35	Cardiff		Wales	D 1-1
13.11.35	Tynecastle		N. Ireland	W 2-1
4.4.36	Wembley		England	D 1-1
14.10.36	Ibrox		Germany	W 2-0
31.10.36	Belfast		N. Ireland	W 3-1
2.12.36	Dens Park		Wales	L 1-2
17.4.37	Hampden		England	W 3-1
9.5.37	Vienna		Austria	D 1-1
15.5.37	Prague		Czech'vakia	W 3-1
30.10.37	Cardiff		Wales	L 1-2
10.11.37	Pittodrie		N. Ireland	D 1-1
8.12.37	Hampden		Czech'vakia	W 5-0
9.4.38	Wembley		England	W 1-0
21.5.38	Amsterdam		Holland	W 3-1
8.10.38	Belfast		N. Ireland	W 2-0
9.11.38	Tynecastle		Wales	W 3-2
7.12.38	Ibrox		Hungary	W 3-1
15.4.39	Hampden		England	L 1-2
19.10.46	Wrexham		Wales	L 1-3
27.11.46	Hampden		N. Ireland	D 0-0
12.4.47	Wembley		England	D 1-1
18.5.47	Brussels		Belgium	L 1-2
24.5.47	Lux'bourg		Lux'bourg	W 6-0
4.10.47	Belfast		N. Ireland	L 0-2
12.11.47	Hampden		Wales	L 1-2
10.4.48	Hampden		England	L 0-2
28.4.48	Hampden		Belgium	W 2-0
17.5.48	Bern		Switzerland	L 1-2
23.5.48	Paris		France	L 0-3
23.10.48	Cardiff		Wales	W 3-1
17.11.48	Hampden		N. Ireland	W 3-2
9.4.49	Wembley		England	W 3-1
27.4.49	Hampden		France	W 2-0
1.10.49	Belfast	*(W)	N. Ireland	W 8-2
9.11.49	Hampden	*(W)	Wales	W 2-0
15.4.50	Hampden	*(W)	England	L 0-1
26.4.50	Hampden		Switzerland	W 3-1
21.5.50	Lisbon		Portugal	D 2-2
27.5.50	Paris		France	W 1-0
21.10.50	Cardiff		Wales	W 3-1
1.11.50	Hampden		N. Ireland	W 6-1
13.12.50	Hampden		Austria	L 0-1
14.4.51	Wembley		England	W 3-2
12.5.51	Hampden		Denmark	W 3-1
16.5.51	Hampden		France	W 1-0
20.5.51	Brussels		Belgium	W 5-0
27.5.51	Vienna		Austria	L 0-4
6.10.51	Belfast		N. Ireland	W 3-0
14.11.51	Hampden		Wales	L 0-1
5.4.52	Hampden		England	L 1-2
30.4.52	Hampden		USA	W 6-0
25.5.52	Copenhagen		Denmark	W 2-1
30.5.52	Stockholm		Sweden	L 1-3
18.10.52	Cardiff		Wales	W 2-1
5.11.52	Hampden		N. Ireland	D 1-1
18.4.53	Wembley		England	D 2-2
6.5.53	Hampden		Sweden	L 1-2
3.10.53	Belfast	*(W)	N. Ireland	W 3-1
4.11.53	Hampden	*(W)	Wales	D 3-3
3.4.54	Hampden	*(W)	England	L 2-4
5.5.54	Hampden		Norway	W 1-0
19.5.54	Oslo		Norway	D 1-1
25.5.54	Helsinki		Finland	W 2-1
16.6.54	Zurich	(W)	Austria	L 0-1
19.6.54	Basel	(W)	Uruguay	L 0-7
16.10.54	Cardiff		Wales	W 1-0
3.11.54	Hampden		N. Ireland	D 2-2
8.12.54	Hampden		Hungary	L 2-4
2.4.55	Wembley		England	L 2-7
4.5.55	Hampden		Portugal	W 3-0
15.5.55	Belgrade		Yugoslavia	D 2-2
19.5.55	Vienna		Austria	W 4-1
29.5.55	Budapest		Hungary	L 1-3
8.10.55	Belfast		N. Ireland	L 1-2
9.11.55	Hampden		Wales	W 2-0
14.4.56	Hampden		England	D 1-1
2.5.56	Hampden		Austria	D 1-1
20.10.56	Cardiff		Wales	D 2-2
7.11.56	Hampden		N. Ireland	W 1-0
21.11.56	Hampden		Yugoslavia	W 2-0
6.4.57	Wembley		England	L 1-2
8.5.57	Hampden	(W)	Spain	W 4-2
19.5.57	Basel	(W)	Switzerland	W 2-1
22.5.57	Stuttgart	(W)	W. Germany	W 3-1
26.5.57	Madrid	(W)	Spain	L 1-4
5.10.57	Belfast		N. Ireland	D 1-1
6.11.57	Hampden	(W)	Switzerland	W 3-2
13.11.57	Hampden		Wales	D 1-1
19.4.58	Hampden		England	L 0-4
7.5.58	Hampden		Hungary	D 1-1
1.6.58	Warsaw		Poland	W 2-1
8.6.58	Vasteras	(W)	Yugoslavia	D 1-1
11.6.58	Norrkoping	(W)	Paraguay	L 2-3
15.6.58	Orebro	(W)	France	L 1-2
18.10.58	Cardiff		Wales	W 3-0
5.11.58	Hampden		N. Ireland	D 2-2
11.4.59	Wembley		England	L 0-1
6.5.59	Hampden		W. Germany	W 3-2
27.5.59	Amsterdam		Holland	W 2-1
3.6.59	Lisbon		Portugal	L 0-1
3.10.59	Belfast		N. Ireland	W 4-0
4.11.59	Hampden		Wales	D 1-1
9.4.60	Hampden		England	D 1-1
4.5.60	Hampden		Poland	L 2-3
29.5.60	Vienna		Austria	L 1-4
5.6.60	Budapest		Hungary	D 3-3
8.6.60	Ankara		Turkey	L 2-4
22.10.60	Cardiff		Wales	L 0-2
9.11.60	Hampden		N. Ireland	W 5-2
15.4.61	Wembley		England	L 3-9
3.5.61	Hampden	(W)	Eire	W 4-1
7.5.61	Dublin	(W)	Eire	W 3-0
14.5.61	Bratislava	(W)	Czech'vakia	L 0-4
26.9.61	Hampden	(W)	Czech'vakia	W 3-2
7.10.61	Belfast		N. Ireland	W 6-1
8.11.61	Hampden		Wales	W 2-0
29.11.61	Brussels	(W)	Czech'vakia	L 2-4
14.4.62	Hampden		England	W 2-0
2.5.62	Hampden		Uruguay	L 2-3
20.10.62	Cardiff		Wales	W 3-2
7.11.62	Hampden		N. Ireland	W 5-1
6.4.63	Wembley		England	W 2-1
8.5.63	Hampden**		Austria	W 4-1
4.6.63	Bergen		Norway	L 3-4
9.6.63	Dublin		Eire	L 0-1
13.6.63	Madrid		Spain	W 6-2
12.10.63	Belfast		N. Ireland	L 1-2
7.11.63	Hampden		Norway	W 6-1
20.11.63	Hampden		Wales	W 2-1
11.4.64	Hampden		England	W 1-0
12.5.64	Hanover		W. Germany	D 2-2
3.10.64	Cardiff		Wales	L 2-3
21.10.64	Hampden	(W)	Finland	W 3-1
25.11.64	Hampden		N. Ireland	W 3-2
10.4.65	Wembley		England	D 2-2
8.5.65	Hampden		Spain	D 0-0
23.5.65	Chorzow	(W)	Poland	D 1-1
27.5.65	Helsinki	(W)	Finland	W 2-1
2.10.65	Belfast		N. Ireland	L 2-3
13.10.65	Hampden	(W)	Poland	L 1-2
9.11.65	Hampden	(W)	Italy	W 1-0
24.11.65	Hampden		Wales	W 4-1
7.12.65	Naples	(W)	Italy	L 0-3
2.4.66	Hampden		England	L 3-4
11.5.66	Hampden		Holland	L 0-3
18.6.66	Hampden		Portugal	L 0-1
25.6.66	Hampden		Brazil	L 1-1
22.10.66	Cardiff	*(E)	Wales	D 1-1
16.11.66	Hampden	*(E)	N. Ireland	W 2-1
15.4.67	Wembley	*(E)	England	W 3-2
10.5.67	Hampden		USSR	L 0-2
21.10.67	Belfast	*(E)	Ireland	L 0-1
22.11.67	Hampden	*(E)	Wales	W 3-2
24.2.68	Hampden	*(E)	England	D 1-1
30.5.68	Amsterdam		Holland	D 0-0
16.10.68	Copenhagen		Denmark	L 0-1
6.11.68	Hampden	(W)	Austria	W 2-1
11.12.68	Nicosia	(W)	Cyprus	W 5-0
16.4.69	Hampden	(W)	W. Germany	D 1-1
3.5.69	Wrexham		Wales	W 5-3
6.5.69	Hampden		N. Ireland	D 1-1
10.5.69	Wembley		England	L 1-4
17.5.69	Hampden	(W)	Cyprus	W 8-0
21.9.69	Dublin		Eire	D 1-1
22.10.69	Hamburg	(W)	W. Germany	L 2-3
5.11.69	Vienna	(W)	Austria	L 0-2
18.4.70	Belfast		N. Ireland	W 1-0
22.4.70	Hampden		Wales	D 0-0
25.4.70	Hampden		England	D 0-0
11.11.70	Hampden	(E)	Denmark	W 1-0
3.2.71	Liege	(E)	Belgium	L 0-3
21.4.71	Lisbon	(E)	Portugal	L 0-2
15.5.71	Cardiff		Wales	D 0-0
18.5.71	Hampden		N. Ireland	L 0-1
22.5.71	Wembley		England	L 1-3
9.6.71	Copenhagen	(E)	Denmark	L 0-1
14.6.71	Moscow		USSR	L 0-1
13.10.71	Hampden	(E)	Portugal	W 2-1
10.11.71	Aberdeen	(E)	Belgium	W 1-0
1.12.71	Amsterdam		Holland	L 1-2
26.4.72	Hampden		Peru	W 2-0
20.5.72	Hampden†		N. Ireland	W 2-0
24.5.72	Hampden		Wales	W 1-0
27.5.72	Hampden		England	L 0-1
28.6.72	B. Horizonte		Yugoslavia	D 2-2

Date	Venue		Country	Result	
2.7.72	Porto Alegre		Czech'vakia	D	0-0
5.7.72	Rio		Brazil	L	0-1
18.10.72	Copenhagen	(W)	Denmark	W	4-1
15.11.72	Hampden	(W)	Denmark	W	2-0
14.2.73	Hampden		England	L	0-5
12.5.73	Wrexham		Wales	W	2-0
16.5.73	Hampden		N. Ireland	L	1-2
19.5.73	Wembley		England	L	0-1
22.6.73	Bern		Switzerland	L	0-1
30.6.73	Hampden		Brazil	L	0-1
26.9.73	Hampden	(W)	Czech'vakia	W	2-1
17.10.73	Bratislava	(W)	Czech'vakia	L	0-1
14.11.73	Hampden		W. Germany	D	1-1
27.3.74	Frankfurt		W. Germany	L	1-2
11.5.74	Hampden†		N. Ireland	L	0-1
14.5.74	Hampden		Wales	W	2-0
18.5.74	Hampden		England	W	2-0
1.6.74	Bruges		Belgium	L	1-2
6.6.74	Oslo		Norway	W	2-1
14.6.74	Dortmund	(W)	Zaire	W	2-0
18.6.74	Frankfurt	(W)	Brazil	D	0-0
22.6.74	Frankfurt	(W)	Yugoslavia	D	1-1
30.10.74	Hampden		E. Germany	W	3-0
20.11.74	Hampden	(E)	Spain	L	1-2
5.2.75	Valencia	(E)	Spain	D	1-1
16.4.75	Gothenburg		Sweden	D	1-1
13.5.75	Hampden		Portugal	W	1-0
17.5.75	Cardiff		Wales	D	2-2
20.5.75	Hampden		N. Ireland	W	3-0
24.5.75	Wembley		England	L	1-5
1.6.75	Bucharest	(E)	Rumania	D	1-1
3.9.75	Copenhagen	(E)	Denmark	W	1-0
29.10.75	Hampden	(E)	Denmark	W	3-1
17.12.75	Hampden	(E)	Rumania	D	1-1
7.4.76	Hampden		Switzerland	W	1-0
6.5.76	Hampden		Wales	W	3-1
8.5.76	Hampden†		N. Ireland	W	3-0
15.5.76	Hampden		England	W	2-1
8.9.76	Hampden		Finland	W	6-0
13.10.76	Prague	(W)	Czech'vakia	L	0-2
17.11.76	Hampden	(W)	Wales	W	1-0
27.4.77	Hampden		Sweden	W	3-1
28.5.77	Wrexham		Wales	D	0-0
1.6.77	Hampden		N. Ireland	W	3-0
4.6.77	Wembley		England	W	2-1
15.6.77	Santiago		Chile	W	4-2
18.6.77	Buenos Aires		Argentina	D	1-1
23.6.77	Rio		Brazil	L	0-2
7.9.77	East Berlin		E. Germany	L	0-1
21.9.77	Hampden	(W)	Czech'vakia	W	3-1
12.10.77	Anfield‡	(W)	Wales	W	2-0
22.2.78	Hampden		Bulgaria	W	2-1
13.5.78	Hampden†		N. Ireland	D	1-1
17.5.78	Hampden		Wales	D	1-1
20.5.78	Hampden		England	L	0-1
3.6.78	Cordoba	(W)	Peru	L	1-3
7.6.78	Cordoba	(W)	Iran	D	1-1
11.6.78	Mendoza	(W)	Holland	W	3-2
20.9.78	Vienna	(E)	Austria	L	2-3
25.10.78	Hampden	(E)	Norway	W	3-2
29.11.78	Lisbon	(E)	Portugal	L	0-1
19.5.79	Cardiff		Wales	L	0-3
22.5.79	Hampden		N. Ireland	W	1-0
26.5.79	Wembley		England	L	1-3
2.6.79	Hampden		Argentina	L	1-3
7.6.79	Oslo	(E)	Norway	W	4-0
12.9.79	Hampden		Peru	D	1-1
17.10.79	Hampden	(E)	Austria	D	1-1
21.11.79	Brussels	(E)	Belgium	L	0-2
19.12.79	Brussels	(E)	Belgium	L	1-3
26.3.80	Hampden	(E)	Portugal	W	4-1
17.5.80	Belfast		N. Ireland	L	0-1
21.5.80	Cardiff		Wales	D	1-1
24.5.80	Hampden		England	L	0-2
28.5.80	Poznan		Poland	L	0-1
31.5.80	Budapest		Hungary	L	1-3
10.9.80	Stockholm	(W)	Sweden	W	1-0
15.10.80	Hampden	(W)	Portugal	D	0-0
25.2.81	Tel Aviv	(W)	Israel	W	1-0
25.3.81	Hampden	(W)	N. Ireland	D	1-1
28.4.81	Hampden	(W)	Israel	W	3-1
16.5.81	Swansea		Wales	L	0-2
19.5.81	Hampden		N. Ireland	W	2-0
23.5.81	Wembley		England	W	1-0
9.9.81	Hampden	(W)	Sweden	W	2-0
14.10.81	Belfast	(W)	N. Ireland	D	0-0
18.11.81	Lisbon	(W)	Portugal	L	1-2
24.2.82	Valencia		Spain	L	0-3
23.3.82	Hampden		Holland	W	2-1
28.4.82	Belfast		N. Ireland	D	1-1
24.5.82	Hampden		Wales	W	1-0
29.5.82	Hampden		England	L	0-1
15.6.82	Malaga	(W)	N. Zealand	W	5-2
18.6.82	Seville	(W)	Brazil	L	1-4
22.6.82	Malaga	(W)	USSR	D	2-2
13.10.82	Hampden	(E)	E. Germany	W	2-0
17.11.82	Berne	(E)	Switzerland	L	0-2
15.12.82	Brussells	(E)	Belgium	L	2-3
30.3.83	Hampden	(E)	Switzerland	D	2-2
24.5.83	Hampden		N. Ireland	D	0-0
28.5.83	Cardiff		Wales	W	2-0
1.6.83	Wembley		England	L	0-2
12.6.83	Vancouver		Canada	W	2-0
16.6.83	Edmonton		Canada	W	3-0
19.6.83	Toronto		Canada	W	2-0
21.9.83	Hampden		Uruguay	W	2-0
12.10.83	Hampden	(E)	Belgium	D	1-1
16.11.83	Halle	(E)	E. Germany	L	1-2
13.12.83	Belfast		N. Ireland	L	0-2
28.2.84	Hampden		Wales	W	2-1
26.5.84	Hampden		England	D	1-1
1.6.84	Marseilles		France	L	0-2

(**W**) World Cup
(**E**) European Nations Cup/European Championship
* Home International Championship doubled as qualifying tournament.
** Abandoned by referee after 79 minutes because of persistent fouling by Austrian players.
† Re-sheduled from Belfast for security reasons.
‡ Switched by Welsh F.A. because of inadequate capacities of available Welsh grounds.

Below: *Jimmy McMullan leads out the "Wembley Wizards", 1928. Jackson, Gallacher and Harkness follow.*

Selected Bibliography

Compiled by Pat Woods

General History and Development

The Scots Book of Football (Wolfe Publishing Ltd., London, 1969)

Scottish Football League Review. Annually; No. 1 1980 — (Scottish Football League, Glasgow)

Aitken (Mike) *ed.: When will we see your like again? The changing face of Scottish football* (EUSPB Edinburgh, 1977)

Anderson (Chalmers) 'Custodian': *Scottish Cup Football 1873-1946* (C.J. Cousland and Sons Ltd., Edinburgh, 1946)

Archer (Ian) and **Royle** (Trevor) *eds.: We'll support you evermore: the impertinent saga of Scottish fitba'* (Souvenir Press, London, 1976)

Crampsey (Bob): *The Scottish Footballer* (Blackwood, Edinburgh, 1978)

Fabian (A.H.) and **Green** (Geoffrey) *eds.: Association Football* (Caxton Publishing Co. Ltd., 4 vols, 1960 — vol. 4, part XV, 12 chapters on "Football in Scotland" by W.G. Gallagher)

Hutchinson (John): *The Football Industry* (Richard Drew Publishing, Glasgow, 1982)

McCartney (John): *Story of the Scottish Football League 1890-1930* (Published by author, Edinburgh, 1930)

McLeod (Rod): *100 Years of the Scottish Football Association* (STV, Glasgow, 1973)

Peebles (Ian) *ed.: S.F.A. Annual.* No. 1 1978 — No. 5 1982 (Clive-Allan Stuart Ltd., Glasgow)

Rafferty (John): *One Hundred Years of Scottish Football* (Pan Books, London, 1973)

Robertson (Forrest) *comp. and ed.: Mackinlay's A-Z of Scottish Football.* New edition (MacDonald Publishers, Loanhead, 1980)

Smailes (Gordon) *comp.: A Record of Scottish League Football — dates, results and final tables, 1890 — 1983. 4 parts* (Association of Football Statisticians, 22 Bretons, Basildon, Essex, 1983)

Soar (Phil) *comp.: The Hamlyn A-Z of British Football Records* (Hamlyn, London, 1981)

Taylor (Hugh): *Great Masters of Scottish Football* (Stanley Paul, London, 1967)

Taylor (Hugh) *ed.: Scottish Football Book.* Annually, No. 1 1955 — No. 28 1982 (Stanley Paul, London). The series is to be revived under the editorship of Ian Archer in 1984.

Club Histories

List of club histories published in book or brochure format only. Certain clubs (e.g. Stirling Albion) have serialised their history (or part of their history) in the club programme. It is worth noting that clubs such as Celtic, Rangers and Queen's Park have had two or more books published on their history and in these cases the most recent publication is listed. Also, since 1969 there have appeared the annuals *Playing for Celtic* and *Playing for Rangers* (Stanley Paul, London) and the Old Firm dominance of the Scottish football publishing sphere is reflected in the fact that virtually all the autobiographies of Scottish club players are those of personalities of Celtic (e.g. Jimmy McGrory, Jimmy Johnstone, Danny McGrain) and Rangers (e.g. Willie Henderson, John Greig, Derek Johnstone). A significant exception to this is Gordon Strachan whose biography appeared in 1984, while he was still with Aberdeen.

Aberdeen: Webster (Jack) *The Dons* (Stanley Paul, London, 1978)

Alloa: Anon. *Alloa through the years* (Simmath Press Ltd., Dundee, 1949)

Arbroath: Gray (Malcolm) and Mylles (Stephen) *The Red Lichties.* Centenary 1878-1978 (Arbroath F.C., 1978)

Ayr United: Hannah (Billy) *The Ayr United Story.* Jubilee, 1910-1960 (Ayr Advertiser, 1960)

Berwick Rangers: Langmack (Tony) *Berwick Rangers, a sporting miracle!* Centenary, 1881-1981 (Berwick Rangers F.C., 1981)

Celtic: McNee (Gerald) *The Story of Celtic, an official history 1888-1978* (Stanley Paul, London, 1978)

Clyde: Greig (Tom) *The Bully Wee.* Centenary, 1877-1977 (Clyde F.C., Glasgow, 1977)

Dundee: Boyne (H.B.) *The Dark Blues Down the Years, the story of Dundee F.C. in word and picture* (Simmath Press Ltd., Dundee, 1948)

Dundee United: H.B.B. (presumably H.B. Boyne) *Dundee United F.C. Through the Years, the history of Dundee United F.C. in word and picture* (Simmath Press, Ltd., Dundee, 1947)

East Fife: Phenix (William) *The History of East Fife* (Simmath Press Ltd., Dundee, 1948)

East Stirlingshire: McMillan (Alan) *Showing in Black and White Only.* Centenary, 1881-1981 (Garrell Press, Kilsyth, 1981)

Falkirk: McFarlane (Willie) *The Bairns.* Centenary, 1876-1976 (Audio Litho, Edinburgh, 1976)

Forfar Athletic: Anon. *The History of Forfar Athletic* (Simmath Press Ltd., Dundee, 1949)

Heart of Midlothian: Mackie (Albert) *The Hearts* (Stanley Paul, London, 1959)
N.B. a small brochure was issued by the club to commemorate the centenary, 1874-1974. Contained brief outline of history

Hibernian: Docherty (Gerry) and Thomson (Phil) *100 Years of Hibs.* Centenary, 1875-1975 (John Donald Publishers Ltd., Edinburgh, 1975)

Kilmarnock: Taylor (Hugh) *Go, fame . . .* Centenary, 1869-1969 (Kilmarnock F.C., 1969)

Montrose: Anon. *The History of Montrose* (Simmath Press Ltd., Dundee, 1948)

Morton: Robertson (Tom) *Morton 1874-1974.* Centenary (Morton F.C., Greenock, 1974)

Partick Thistle: Archer (Ian) *The Jags.* Centenary, 1876-1976 (Molendinar Press, Glasgow, 1976)

Queen of the South: Jardine (W.) *The Queens 1919-1969.* Jubilee (Standard Press, Dumfries, 1969)

Queen's Park: Crampsey (R.A.) *The Game for the Game's Sake.* Centenary, 1867-1967 (Queen's Park F.C., Glasgow, 1967)

Raith Rovers: Litster (John) *Raith Rovers.* Centenary, 1883-1983 (Raith Rovers F.C., Kirkcaldy, 1983)

Rangers: Peebles (Ian) *Growing with Glory.* Centenary, 1873-1973 (Rangers F.C., Glasgow, 1973)

St. Mirren: Hunter (Willie) *The Saints.* Centenary, 1877-1977. (Paisley Daily Express, 1977)

Stenhousemuir: Moulds (Peter) *The Warriors.* Centenary, 1884-1984 (Stenhousemuir F.C., 1984)

Stranraer: Boyd (John S.) ed. *Stranraer F.C.* Centenary, 1870-1970 (Free Press, Stranraer, 1970)

International Competition

Glanville (Brian): *The History of the World Cup.* Revised edition (Faber and Faber, London, 1980)

James (Brian): *England v. Scotland.* (Pelham Books, London, 1969)

Lamming (Douglas), *comp.: Who's Who of Scottish Internationalists, 1872-1982.* In 4 parts, A-Z (Association of Football Statisticians, 22 Bretons, Basildon, Essex, 1982)

Soar (Phil) and Widdows (Richard): *Spain '82* (Hamlyn, London, 1982)

European Club Competition

MacDonald (Roger): *Britain versus Europe* (Pelham Books, London, 1968)

Motson (John) and Rowlinson (John): *The European Cup, 1955-1980* (Queen Anne Press, London, 1980)

Humour

Fairgrieve (John): *Away wi' the goalie!* (Stanley Paul, London, 1977)

Pat Woods, compiler of *Celtic F.C. Facts and Figures 1888-1981* (1981), is both a football fan and a student of the history, particularly social history, of the game.

Index

For reasons of space players in team photographs have not been indexed individually.

Page numbers in bold type refer to illustrations.

Football seasons are referred to by the second year of the season: for example, (1984) = season 1983-84.

Hamish Whyte